Lights of Fire

The Harrowing Mystery of the Dyatlov Pass Incident

Lights of Fire

The Harrowing Mystery of the Dyatlov Pass Incident

Jack Randle

Copyright © 2021 by Jack Randle.

Parchment Global Publishing
1500 Market Street, 12th Floor, East Tower
Philadelphia, Pennsylvania, 19102
www.parchmentglobalpublishing.com

ISBN 978-1-952302-18-3 (sc)
ISBN 978-1-952302-19-0 (e)

Library of Congress Control Number: 2020915017

All rights reserved. No part of this book may be reproduced, stored, or transmitted by any means—whether auditory, graphic, mechanical, or electronic—without written permission of both publisher and author, except in the case of brief excerpts used in critical articles and reviews. Unauthorized reproduction of any part of this work is illegal and is punishable by law.

CONTENTS

The Dyatlov Pass Incident 1

Mystery of Their Actions and Final Resting Places 5

The Hikers Names, History, and Cause of Death 10

The Strange Lights in the Sky 23

The Dyatlov Trip to Dead Mountain 26

Opening The Door? 32

Brief History of Bible and Strong's Dictionary 43

Gideon's Lamps 49

Passover / After the Manner of Egypt 57

David's Numbering 64

The Angels of Sodom and Gomorrah 67

The Four Horns of Slaughter 70

INTRODUCTION

The theory in this book comes straight from the horse's mouth, to use an old idiomatic expression. It was the beginning of the year 2013 and New York has just dropped the ball and set off its fireworks. Across the countryside, some of the local pyrotechnic explosions still lit the night sky to welcome the New Year. The house in which I lived in at that time sits on top of a hill with a panoramic view of about 180 degrees and you could see far into the distance. A half hour past midnight the fireworks were coming to an end, and things were starting to quiet down. Out of the corner of my eye, I saw an orange-red object moving from the west side of the valley. It appeared to be about 25 feet in circumference, but it wasn't exactly a round object like a ball. As this object moved directly in my line of sight, it illuminated the clouds which were low that night. It kept moving towards the east side of the valley and suddenly it went up into the clouds and disappeared.

Coast to Coast is a radio program that airs at 1 A.M. in my area. The host of the program, George Noory, reports inexplicable news that other news organizations don't. After settling in New Year's morning, I got ready for my routine of listening to the news about what is going on around the world. George Noory reported that people were seeing orbs up and down the east coast of the United States. He said that they were seeing as many as six orbs in some areas. George's report is the first instance where I heard anybody talk about orbs in a way that I understood what they were seeing because I just encountered one. It's human nature to just dismiss something like that, because how can you explain a ball of light floating across the sky?

I later told some people what I saw, and some suggested that (1) I saw some kind of Chinese lantern. However, it moved faster than a hot air balloon that I've seen around the countryside many times. Hot air balloons make a whoosh sound from the fire ignition when they want to rise, but there was no sound from this object when it went up. (2) Some say it could have been an airplane, because when an airplane comes straight towards you, the lights appear to be standing still for a long time. But after it makes a turn, then you can see it's an airplane. Also, no airplane can get close without making a sound or move around like that, so the object could not have been a plane. (3) Some also told me that I saw a meteor, but meteors don't move like that before going up into the clouds. It's understandable why people dismiss it when you tell them something like that because there's an old saying, "seeing is believing." With these reports, it made me feel more confident about what I saw knowing other people were seeing orbs that night also.

About a month or so later, someone where I worked told me that a horse named Orb was looking to head for the Kentucky Derby. I thought it was a strange name for a horse, so I told him that I saw an orb and that Orb would win the Kentucky Derby. Like when certain numbers come up, people will play those numbers based on experience. Lots of three-year-old horses want to get into the Kentucky Derby, but to say that a horse would win at that time would've been a long shot; so I didn't really believe he would win. After a horse gets in the Kentucky Derby, there are at least 20 other horses that he has to beat; so I chalked the name up to being merely a coincidence. On the first Saturday in May, this horse named Orb won the 2013 Kentucky Derby. After that happened, I started thinking there must be more to the orb experience. It's a hard thing for me to believe in coincidences when it comes to a phenomenon like that!

In the Old Testament, there was a man named Oreb. Being close to the word orb, I looked into what was written about him. That took me to Isaiah Chapter 10 Verse 26 in the King James Version where it speaks of the slaughter of Midian at the rock of Oreb after the manner of Egypt. "Slaughter of Midian…"; "At the rock of Oreb…"; "After the manner of Egypt…". These are three very important phrases in that verse that will be discussed in later chapters. Also as "coincidence" would have it, mysterious deaths which include the talk of orbs would catch my ear regarding the Dyatlov Pass incident. George Noory had the author of *Dead Mountain* by Donnie Eichar, on his radio show. When they spoke about these orbs and the mystery of nine Russian hikers; I bought his book. His book speaks of this mystery as well as the history of Russia during the time of the event. A very good read!

Then at the beginning of 2017, I read the book *Dyatlov Pass Keeps Its Secrets*, by Irina and Vlad Lobatchev and Amanda Bosworth. This book described more of the autopsies of the bodies and gave more mysteries surrounding the event. It convinced me that there was more to what happened that New Year's night. This truly was the mystery of all mysteries. Again both books are very good reads and had a part in inspiring me to write a theory on the orb sightings. In *Dead Mountain*, on a page behind the table of contents, is a question by Yuri Yudin. "If I could ask God just one question it would be what really happened to my friends that night?" In *Dyatlov Pass Keeps Its Secrets*, pages 158 and 159 there's a statement that says: "As you have noticed by now, the book does not delve into the discussion of the supernatural causes of the Dyatlov group tragedy. Maybe the Dyatlov Pass was a place where a paranormal occurrence took place or maybe it was the Soviet Roswell - Russian community of amateur investigators awaits your ideas and expertise." Since I do not believe in coincidences with this phenomenon, and since both books spurred me to write about a theory that aligns and relates with Biblical inspirations, I decided to do just that. I was moved to write a book when a publisher contacted me about my copyrighted theory. My original intent for copyrighting this theory was to find a movie producer who would produce it and stay within the conjectures and documented facts of the case, as much as possible.

"Take ye heed: Behold, I have foretold you all things." (Mark 13:23) K.J.V.

Special thanks go to our Creator up above by which none of these would've been possible without Him bringing the importance of the orb events to my attention!

THE DYATLOV PASS INCIDENT

Dead Mountain is a mountain in Russia, so called because there are no trees growing on it. At the elevation of 1079 meters, is where the mysteries began. They reevaluated the elevations since then, but it is still referred to as the 1079. The temperatures reach -30° below zero or more, with hurricane force winds in the winter. February 1, 1959, a one of a kind, horrifying event unfolded in the Northern Urals of Russia where nine Russian hikers did not return. They sent out a search party to look for them. The missing group had been made up of seven men, and two women.

This is what they discovered…February 26, 1959, they found the tent with an ice ax beside it, so the search team used it to force their way in. After they hacked their way in, they felt relief for a moment because there were no bodies inside. As the searchers looked around, it appeared as though the hikers may return at any time. A napkin with slices of ham, an open flask of cocoa sitting nearby were it was left as though it was waiting to be reheated, and the surrounding arrangements give the impression the hikers will soon return.

However, the searchers realized there was something very wrong with the scene before them. Coats and blankets lay on the floor. The boots were lined up along the wall inside of the tent. No one in their right mind would leave the tent without putting on the things they would need for their survival in such a brutal environment. These were very intelligent, experienced hikers who were going for a grade 3 certification; the highest certification in the country at the time. It was taken so seriously that the tenth hiker returned home early because of health problems. He returned since he didn't want to be a liability to the other hikers. As much as he wanted to continue on and achieve that goal, he abandoned the dream with the disappointment similar to one who is passing up the opportunity of being on a championship sports team. The remaining hikers continued towards their destination. They dug out a foundation for their tent, getting it well anchored in the very brutal weather conditions. After getting it more secure, it looks as though they were all inside getting ready to set up the stove; seeing that there was food around the vicinity, it looked like they were preparing to eat. And for whatever reason it seemed they stopped what they were doing, took a knife and cut their way out of the tent. Walking away without taking their boots or coats. Searchers found clear, well distinguishable footprints that went down the slope. Evidence suggests they were moving along on foot in an orderly fashion, hand-in-hand. The appearance of the footprints puzzled researchers the most, it was as if they were all in a chain combing the slope possibly looking for something small. Those who investigated the scene could not think of any intelligible reason for this pattern of movement. One man, it seems, had been walking totally barefoot while the others had only socks and felt boots. There were some rocky strips on the slope where the footprints would temporarily disappear, then reappear. Investigators found that two groups of footprints were parted for a brief distance before reuniting; a larger group of about six or seven, and another group leaving two pairs of footprints about 20 meters to the left. They merged again about 30 to 40 meters down the slope without separating again. Loose snow blew away from the compacted snow of the footprints, so all of this was well preserved. This evidence remained intact from February 1 till at least February 27, 1959, which was itself rather odd with the strong winds and snowstorms always present in the area. Considering that this started out as a rescue mission, the actions taken by the search team compromised the investigation a little; but investigators agree that there were no other footprints in the area at the time these hikers went missing. They also agree that there was no sign of a struggle inside or outside the tent. Urine from one of the hikers was found outside the tent. A coat hangs at the entrance of the tent belonging to the leader of the group which had about 800 rubles in the top pocket. Backpacks with their documents, diaries, money, camera, and other stuff were all still inside the tent. The forensics determined that the tent was cut from the inside, which indicates they were in a hurry to get out of their tent. Investigators said they found only one piece of firewood outside and behind the rear wall. A flashlight belonging to one of the hikers was found about 100 meters down from the tent. The switch was on, and the battery was dead. The hikers kept diaries and documented their encounters of each day before retiring for the night, but no entries were made on February 1, 1959.

SOURCE: Wikimedia Commons

February 26, 1959 - Investigators found the hikers' tent with an axe beside it.

MYSTERY OF THEIR ACTIONS AND FINAL RESTING PLACES

The hikers' bizarre walk down the slope without their boots and coats, was not the only thing that puzzled investigators. From February 27, 1959, until the beginning of May, it took almost two months until they found all the bodies. These are some of the things they uncovered. Investigators hypothesize the nine hikers reached their 1079 tent site around 3:00 PM and began digging and clearing out ice and snow for their tent floor. With the ice ax, they were able to level out an area on the slope. The hikers then laid their skis down over the area to set up and anchor the tent on top. After they were in the tent, they started unpacking things and organizing everything for the night. The stove sat in the middle of the tent, it was not yet assembled. Investigators believe it was about 9:00 PM when the hikers started cutting their way out of the tent. The hikers walked straight to a cedar tree 1.5 kilometers away; during a clear day with good visibility, the top of that tree could be seen from the camp site. They lit a bonfire from cedar twigs and branches about 8 centimeters thick. Experts figure it must've been burning for about two hours because half of the branches were burned through. Two of the hikers were found under the cedar tree and were almost naked; their bodies had severe burns. The undergarments and shirts they had been wearing were charred as were some other clothes scattered around the bonfire. Branches on the cedar tree were broken about 5 meters up the tree as though somebody climbed it, and fell, breaking the branches on the way down. One body was face up and the other body was face down with arms spread loosely to the side. It looked as though someone in the group undressed them and took their clothes since there was no evidence of a struggle, the nude bodies were set down next to each other with the appearance of respect. They found three other bodies in a line, looking as if they were trying to make it back to the tent. The first of the three bodies heading in that direction was that of the group leader. He was face up with his left hand to his face. The investigators also noted that there was ice on his face in a way that indicated that he had initially lied face down, melting the snow then having it refreeze to his face. It is also impossible to die with hands clenched into fists and raised in front of your face in the position that investigators found him. Someone must have turned him over on his back after he developed rigor mortis that night.

His body was the first of three hikers found 300 meters away from the Cedar tree. Another body higher up the slope was found underneath 12 -15 centimeters of snow. His body was lying face down with his head toward the tent, clenching his right hand into a fist against his chest, his left arm spread out to the side, and his right leg tucked up under his belly. This hiker was the only one that had 5 - 7 centimeters of ice under his body. Investigator's assumed he'd been alive and unconscious for several hours and the heat from his body, causing the snow to melt then refreeze again. The body was about midway between the other two bodies on the slope, 180 meters up from the group leader, and 150 meters below the next body on the slope. The third body on the slope and closest to the tent was that of a woman. She laid 330 meters up from the first body, that of the group leader, a total of about 600 meters from the cedar tree, this was about 900 meters below the tent. Dense crusted snow covered her body. It seemed she was crawling up the hill, her face covered in blood. Her top layer of pants was undone on both sides, and the rest of her clothes were unbuttoned. Her hands indicated that she was using them long after they were frostbitten. It would be about another two months prior to investigators finding the other four bodies.

The snow whips into the valley like a wind tunnel coming down off the slope. The snow was up to about six meters in depth which made it almost impossible to find their bodies in the ravine. In the beginning of May, they noticed sprigs from young fir trees showing up in a path down into the ravine. They found a pair of pants lying along the path that were severely burned with the right leg cut off by a knife. When they came to the place where the broken sprigs ended, the searchers started digging. They dug down and found a floor about three square meters in size and about a foot above the snow covered ground. Though there were no corpses found on the flooring, they did find four piles of items lying on the floor, as though they marked where four people had sat. About six meters downstream from the floor, they found the body of a woman. She was on her knees resting against the side of a two-foot tall waterfall, her arms raised up around her head, which was resting on a rock. She wore cotton pants that were torn and burned, two woolen socks on her right foot, and a burnt, beige sweater wrapped around her left foot. Another man lay across the top of the waterfall where the woman was found. Above him lay the other two men in a chest-to-back position and lying in the creek. These last four bodies were found 50 meters away from the cedar tree where the first two bodies had been found. They all needed to be dug out from under approximately two and a half meters of snow, and they all were lying in the creek. One man was noted to have burn marks on his hands. The investigators believe he had gone back to the cedar tree and brought the clothes down to this newly built floor. One man had a diary in one hand and a pencil in the other. One of the investigators was said to have asked, "How is it that a man intends to write something, and then ends up in the creek?" Even if the hiker had stood on the ice and had fallen through, the first human instinct is to grab hold of something to slow one's fall. Clearly, he held onto the diary and pencil instead. They figure whatever happened that night, it lasted from 9:00 PM to 3:00 AM. The timing of their deaths was determined from the time of their last meal. With all that seems to have happened that night, it was most likely a six-hour event. Photographs were taken of the bodies before they were removed and taken back for further forensic investigations. Some of these pictures are easily found under the "Dyatlov Pass Incident," on the Internet.

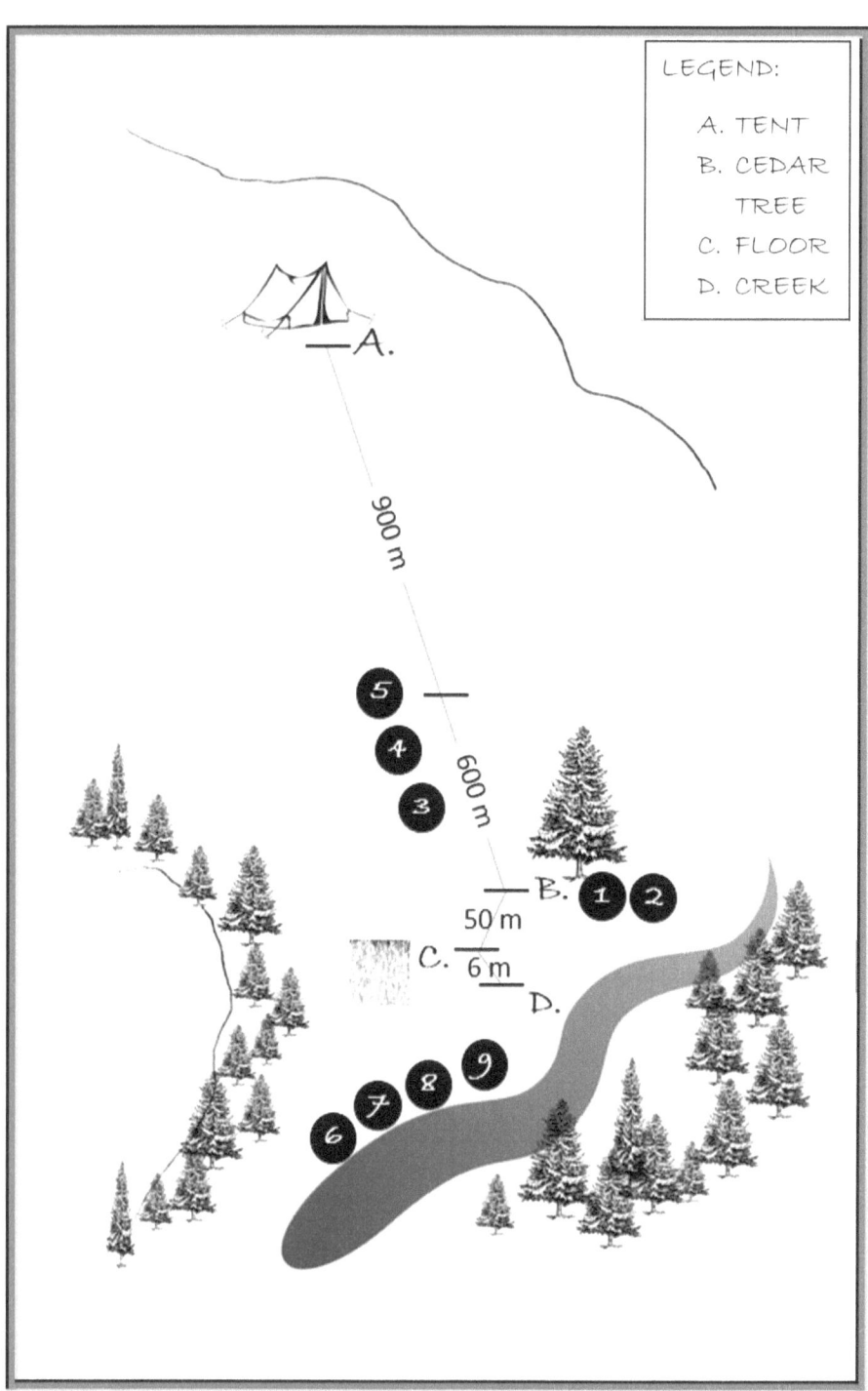

BODY LOCATIONS

1. Yuri (Georgy) Krivonishchenko
2. Yuri Deroshenko
3. Igor Dyatlov
4. Rustem (Rustik) Slobodin
5. Zinaida (Zina) Kolmogorova
6. Lyudmila (Lyuda) Dubinina
7. Nikolay (Kolya) Thibault-Brignoles
8. Alexander (Semyon) Zelotaryov
9. Alexander Kolevatov

THE HIKERS NAMES, HISTORY, AND CAUSE OF DEATH

It was the end of the 1950s; Stalin died; and summer tourism and hiking was gaining extreme popularity among the youth in Russia. The Northern and Southern Urals were the most attractive places for ski routes. At the time, in the central and southern Urals of Russia, the intensity of building factories for the production of weapons grade uranium and plutonium, and the mass manufacturing of nuclear weapons, was escalating. It was the start of the nuclear arms race with the United States of America. Most of the nine hikers went to UPI, Ural Polytechnic Institute. They studied at UPI, which educated and trained engineers for the local industry. They were all Grade 2 hikers embarking on this trip to the Northern Urals for a Grade 3 certification, the highest certification in the country during that time.

Yuri Yudin, 22, a senior student at UPI in the engineering and economics program. The only one of the hikers to survive because of an acute attack of rheumatism which caused him to return home early. Everybody needed to pull their own weight and work together like a well-oiled machine, and he was not going to be the reason they didn't get their Grade 3 certification. (1937-2013)

Igor Dyatlov, 22, was the leader of the group and a talented student in the fifth and the final year of UPI's engineering program. He was considered one of the most experienced sports-skiers among the UPI students. He took part in nine hikes of which he also headed several. Igor developed the final route which the group embarked on. Igor was a strong-willed and intelligent young man, and fellow students considered it an honor to join his group. He invited into this team, friends and tourists he knew well from previous trips.

Several summers earlier, Igor was with a group of hikers when he and his friends encountered a herd of wild horses, an incident documented in the group's journal:

"Suddenly, from behind comes a powerful roar of some unknown origin, but approaching very quickly. We look back and freeze in terror, heading towards us is a herd of wild horses--many, many of them, a whole bunch! The first thought is run! But where to? Igor commands firmly, 'Stop! Nobody move!'" We gather in a tight group, some covering their eyes, others with eyes wide open in horror, watching in complete silence. The herd of about thirty horses racing towards us at full speed! About fifteen meters before they smash into us, the herd suddenly splits into two, and without slowing down, streams all around us, like the river around a rock, and continues on its way.

This is an example of Igor's quick thinking and nerves of steel, his forceful command keeping the group from running to and fro, and the reason why hikers found it an honor to be in his group. He was a person they could learn the skills of survival from. The searchers found Dyatlov's body 300 meters from the cedar tree. He was the first of three bodies on the slope looking as if they were trying to get back to the tent. He had ice on his face from snow melt and then re-freezing. He was lying face up with his hands raised up in front of his face, looking as if he was trying to block the wind. It was clear to investigators that somebody turned him over after he developed rigor mortis that night. Igor died of hypothermia. He had abrasions on his face, hand, and shin; most likely from sliding on the crusted snow.

Rustem (Rustik) Slobodin, 23, was a graduate of UPI and an engineer in a secret nuclear facility in Chelyabinsk. He was probably the most athletic and hardy man in the group as Rustik was a marathoner. Rustik died of hypothermia, aggravated by intracranial brain injury and complicated by subdural hematoma of about seventy-five millimeters in volume. Extensive hemorrhages in the right and left temporal muscles.

A crack in the left temporal bone of the skull up to six centimeters in length. Gaps in some skull sutures on both sides of the head. Hemorrhage on the upper right eyelid, and traces of blood discharge from his nose. His head was almost entirely disfigured. The injuries were made by an unyielding object similar to the crushing force of a well-padded vise. There were no puncture wounds or marks like caused by rocks or a club. It also could not have happened from a simple fall; which the natural, human instinct, is to break the fall with your hands. He had no signs of injury on his limbs that would've been present from that kind of force. Investigators think that he must've been walking in water because his feet looked like they had been partially submerged in water for a time. They found his body, midway between the other two bodies on the slope. 180 meters from Dyatlov and 150 meters from Zina. He had 5 - 7 centimeters of ice under his body.

Zinaida (Zina) Kolmogorova, 22, a senior student in the same program as Igor, a ringleader of any difficult task, and often considered the heart of any team. Zina was wanted by all tourist groups on any route. Her face had been covered in blood, and it looked as though she had struggled to climb back up the slope with frostbitten hands. Investigators believe that the abrasions on her body came from sliding on the ice crusted snow. Her body was found 330 meters from Dyatlov, and about 600 meters from the cedar tree; she was the closest person to the tent and was covered in the ice crusted snow. Zina also died of hypothermia.

Yuri (Georgy) Krivonishchenko, 24, was a graduate of UPI and a foreman for a construction company in Chelyabinsk, a secret town in which the production of weapons grade plutonium was located. Georgy was a close friend of Igor. Georgy died of hypothermia. He had severe burns and frostbites massive in size. It appears as though he fell on top of the fire since his long underwear and shirt were burned. There were also other burnt garments scattered in the area. He had a lot of abrasions and skin wounds, including on his forehead and left temple. His ear, nose, and lips were covered in blood. He was one of the first two hikers found; he was lying face up under the Cedar tree and under light snow.

Yuri Doroshenko, 21, was a student of UPI and worked in an industrial machine department. He was a brave and reliable young man. Yuri died of hypothermia, having severe frostbitten fingers and toes. He had abrasions, scratches, cuts, and bruises on the shoulder, forearms, hands, and front surfaces of both legs. He also had nasal and ear bleeding as well as blood on the lips. Forensic experts found foamy gray fluid coming from the opening of his mouth and in his lungs. They gave no comment on the origin of the liquid. Some investigators with medical backgrounds suggest that it may have been caused by a seizure or by choking from an intense squeezing of the chest. He had severe burns on his body, clothes, long underwear, and shirt. His body was lying with Georgy, face down under the Cedar tree and under light snow. Some witnesses who saw the remains said their skin color looked strange, orange-brown.

Source: Russian National Files

Yuri Krivonischenko and Yuri Doroshenko

Two months would pass before they find the other four bodies. These first five hikers all died of hypothermia; and, with the exception of Rustem Slobodin, they could've all survived that night if they hadn't frozen to death. Before covering details of the next four hikers found 50 meters further into the ravine, it may be time to cover several theories to this point.

1. There were some who wanted to chalk these bizarre signs up to an avalanche before they found the next four bodies. Some of the investigators in Russia knew it wasn't adding up to an avalanche, even before finding the next four bodies. They had to walk about 1.5 kilometers, or 1,500 meters from the tent to the cedar tree, so the obvious question to ask with that theory: How far do you walk down that slope before you realize you need to try to get back to the tent and warmer clothes? And the key word is: walk. The tent was not wiped out or pushed off its foundation by snow. It would be a natural assumption that Igor didn't want to worry about the strong winds bringing an avalanche down on them while they sleep. The theory of an avalanche is more of an embarrassment which it may make it easier than searching for the truth, but it doesn't fit the signs.

2. Then there was a theory of them being drunk, which has its own difficulties! You have nine intelligent hikers going for a Grade 3 certification. This would have given them a lot of prestige among other hikers in Russia. These hikers already had a Grade 2 certification, so we can be sure they were serious about hiking. How do you get Igor Dyatlov, and the other seven experienced hikers to go along with an uncontrolled drinking binge? If they would've survived, it could have brought about some serious consequences for Dyatlov Group.

3. Some were blaming the Mansi tribe, or some escaped convicts from a local work camp, for their deaths; but most investigators quickly ruled this theory out. The obvious question with that theory are: Where were all the footprints of intruders who managed to overcome nine hikers, and why cut your way out of the tent and walk away without boots and coats? A camera, money, and alcohol were some of the items left at the tent untouched.

One more theory could be said to make the most common sense, before disclosing the mysteries of the next four hikers.

4. Infrasound generated by a Karman vortex street wind event. This could be produced by two F2 tornadoes passing the tent on either side. Some governments use infrasonic frequencies to disperse crowds, so this theory is that the infrasonic frequencies robbed all the hikers of their rational mind set. The theory says that the infrasonic sounds can affect people differently, but the question that needs to be asked is: Without the hikers having rational thoughts, why did they not all do different things? Why were they not walking all different directions, and why did not one or two just put blankets over their heads and stay put on the tent floor? Igor Dyatlov would›ve known as soon as the hikers were not rational thinking, and being outside in that condition, it would only lead to chaos and death in that unforgiving environment. This of course is assuming that all nine hikers didn't go instantly insane by the infrasonic frequency, along with Igor being in his right mind, by not picking an avalanche area to set the tent. The example of the wild horses shows that he was able to think quickly and had too much instinct for survival for a circumstance like that to catch him off guard. Quick thinking enough to prevent the frequencies havoc of insanity, before it can happen to everyone. Even if the Russian government had the technology and the desire to use infrasonic sound to herd them down into the Lozva valley, the signs don't truly bear this out. An orderly walk instead of a chaotic run while falling over rocks and breaking arms and legs. And the bone-crushing skull injury that Rustem sustained could not have happened by a simple fall, even if he ran! The signs of rock scrapes, cuts, and skin punctures were not there; and he had injuries on both sides of his head. With infrasonic sound responses being different with everyone, it would seem that the cold would outweigh the pain of the infrasonic sound. At least some would have returned to the tent before walking even 50 meters down that slope.

Zina was about 900 meters away from it. Also, why would the Russian government want to lose people who were helping with advancing their nuclear goals? They could have experimented with less valuable people. Though two F2 tornadoes producing infrasonic sound, which caused all nine hikers to walk rather far before deciding to work their way back may be the best theory, but it still doesn't fit the signs of what happened that night. This last theory gives more respect to the nine hiker's intelligences; but before moving on to the next four hikers, it should be noted that there is still another strange phenomenon with this mystery. It's the same phenomenon that Christ spoke of in Matthew 16: 2-3, when He said, "you say when it is evening it will be fair weather: for the sky is red. And in the morning, it will be bad weather today: for the sky is red." "How is it you can discern the sky, but you can't discern the signs of the times?"

The old saying of today is, "red sky at night sailors delight," and "red sky in the morning sailors warning." And it's the same strange thing today with people not being able to discern the signs that are before them with this mystery. There were no signs of Mansi, criminals, animals, Russian soldiers, or American soldiers. There were no signs of an avalanche, hurricane force winds, or meteors. And as for the things that can't be seen, like infrasonic sound, demon possession, or anything else that would cause them to lose rational behavior, there were no signs of panic, or disorientation in those footprints left behind. Everything they did that night was rational and done for good reasons. If we remember the 9 hikers' skills and intelligence, and the investigators conclusion of it being "An Unknown Compelling Force," then we should realize those theories fall short of explaining all the signs around the mystery.

Now we can return to the remaining hikers yet to be found.

The beginning of May, two months since the first five bodies were found, searchers start seeing tree sprigs showing up from under the melting snow. The sprig trail went from the cedar tree in a southwesterly direction towards the ravine. When they reached the end of the sprigs trail, about 50 meters from the cedar tree, they dug down and found a constructed floor. Six meters from this constructed floor, they found the remaining four bodies in a creek.

Alexander Kolevatov, 24, was a senior student of UPI and was in the physics and technology department. Before becoming a UPI student, he worked as a senior technician in the secret nuclear facility in Moscow. His death was likely as a result of an acute heart failure (cardiac arrest). He had a broken nose, a small deep wound behind his right ear, burn marks on his hands and sleeves, and an old bruise around his left knee. He had a bandage on his leg in which he had apparently hurt a few days earlier. The other three bodies did not have bandages on their wounds. Alexander was the only one of the four who did not have any internal injuries. He had on a jacket, two sweaters, a cowboy shirt, fleece underwear, long underwear, ski pants, canvas overalls, two pair of socks, and one more sock unpaired. A box of matches, a piece of wrapping paper, and a pack of codeine pills were found in his pockets. He was the only one with skin burns. This led investigators to believe that he was the only one at the fire under the cedar tree. None of the four had any frostbite on their hands, and their deaths were not caused by hypothermia. Alexander Kolevatov and Semyon Zolotaryov laid together in the creek chest to back when they were found.

Nikolay (Kolya) Thibault-Brignoles, 25, was a graduate of UPI and worked as a foreman in Sverdlovsk. Tourism was his passion in life. Kolya was energetic and friendly and had a great sense of humor. His death was due to traumatic brain injury. A bone fracture on the right side of his skull where the temporal bone bulged into the cranial cavity. He had a diffuse hemorrhage in the right temporal muscle and a 17-centimeter long crack at the base of the skull. There was a 10 x 12 centimeter green-blue bruise on his front right shoulder. His skin was not torn, cut, or punctured. His injury was caused by compression against an unyielding object. His corpse was entirely underwater for some time in the creek, and he was found above the two-foot waterfall.

Alexander (Semyon) Zolotaryov, 37, was the oldest of the group and joined at the last moment. He had a strong military background with four combat awards. He worked as a tourism instructor in the Caucus Mountains. Semyon died on the eve of his birthday of internal bleeding, respiratory failure due to lung edema, and acute heart failure (cardiac arrest). He had double fractures of five ribs on the right side with hemorrhages in the adjacent intercostal muscles. About one liter of blood was in the pleural cavity. He had a wound on his head that exposed the parietal bone, probably from a rock or ice and both of his eyeballs were missing. The broken ribs were caused by an intense force of compression. When they pulled Semyon up, they found a notebook in one hand and a pencil in the other hand. His corpse was entirely underwater for some time in the creek with Alexander Kolevatov, chest to back.

Source: Public Domain

The snowed-out corpses of Kolevatov and Zolotaryov

Lyudmila (Lyuda) Dubinina, 21, was a third-year student in UPI and was in the engineering and economics program. In the winter of 1958, she led a group of skiers on a hike to the Northern Urals. Lyuda liked ice dancing, amateur shows, and singing. Lyuda died of internal bleeding, respiratory failure, cardiac contusion, shock from the pain, and a blockade of respiratory movements. They estimate that she didn't live more than ten minutes after the injury was incurred. She had a hemorrhage in the right ventricle of her heart, multiple rib fractures on both sides of her chest, and defused bruising on her left thigh. She had a missing upper lip, tongue, lower teeth, and eyes. Her hyoid bone and thyroid cartilage had unusual mobility. Some investigators believe the mobility may have come from a blow to the throat or from strangulation. What happened to her missing tongue was impossible for investigators to determine. It was not cut out; and no fish or mice under the snow could've eaten it, because the bodies were frozen like stone until the thawing in May. She was on her knees at the side of the two-foot waterfall, with raised hands around her head. Her head lay face down on a rock. She wore cotton pants that were torn and burnt and a burnt sweater wrapped around her left foot. The other three hikers laid above the waterfall up the creek from her. A fact about these bone crushing injuries with Lyudmila, Nikolay, Semyon, and Rustem, the man found on the slope going up to the tent, was that they were injuries equivalent to that which happens in a car accident of sixty kilometers per hour. They were all alive when they received the injuries, since they suffered hemorrhaging.

Source: Russian National Archives

These last four bodies puzzled investigators with a lot of new questions. These are a few questions that come to mind. 1. After cutting the trees for the floor that made a sprig trail down into the ravine, why didn't

Yuri Doroshenko and George Krivonischenko go along with them into the ravine and out of the wind instead of staying at the Cedar tree and freezing to death? 2. Alexander Kolevatov, 24, had no life-threatening injuries, nor was he overcome by hypothermia. He was dressed rather warm compared to some of the other hikers. How is it that he would end up down at the creek with the other three hikers? 3. Burnt clothes that Alexander probably brought back from the fire under the cedar tree ended up on the floor on four piles. And Lyuda was wearing clothes that were burnt. It would be logical to assume they knew Georgy and Yuri were dead. Why leave the floor this late in the event that night after getting more clothes? 4. Investigators were unable to determine what caused those bone crushing injuries which normally would be caused by a force equivalent to a sixty-kilometer-per-hour accident. How did they come in contact with this bone crushing force of an unyielding object while Alexander did not get the same injuries? 5. They were six meters away from floor. Why was Zolotarev holding a diary in one hand and a pencil in the other while moving out on another hike? Why didn't he do his writing while sitting on the floor?

Like stated earlier, investigators said Lyuda would not have lived for more than ten minutes after receiving her injuries. So it is safe to say that those injuries did not happen up at the tent, and more than likely that Rustem wasn't walking around the mountain side with his head injury either. It would then be logical to say that those injuries happened not far from their last position. From the reports about the floor in the ravine, it stayed pretty much intact, so there was not much reason to leave that floor, to start walking through snow in total darkness, even with a flashlight. In their diary on January 30, they made a note about the struggle they had, walking through the woods; and that would've been in the light of day.

Helicopter pilots working with the search and rescue team were so frightened by the bodies that they refused to evacuate the corpses from the mountain without special packing. It took some time to move the bodies to Ivdel for the autopsies which would've brought retribution if there wasn't a good reason. Also, there are reports that more precautions were taken after doing the autopsies. *Dyatlov Pass Keeps Its Secrets* covers more reports around this event along with resources, names, and pictures.

Source: Wikimedia Commons

The hikers, memorial tomb at the Mikhailovskoe Cemetery in Russia.

THE STRANGE LIGHTS IN THE SKY

In the beginning of February 1959, hikers to Mt. Chistop, the northern Ural which is about 25 kilometers away from Mt. Otorten, noticed a rocket flair in the black sky over the snowy white dome of Mt. Otorten. It puzzled them because the area was wild and unpopulated. The Dyatlov hiking group officially obtained a permit to follow that route from the Sverdlovsk Tourist Club; their hike to take place around the time those rocket flairs were sited. Had any secret trials been planned for that area, the KGB would have banned the route without explanation. After the Dyatlov tragedy, the area was closed to tourism for three years.

Criminalist-prosecutor Lev Ivanov collected testimonies about some strange luminous fireballs in the sky on the northern Ural in winter/spring of 1959. He also suspected them to be rockets.

Eyewitnesses observed the fireballs in the sky over the Northern Ural twice; on February 17 and March 31, 1959. On February 17, 1959, Vladislav Karelin, a member of the search and rescue team and the vice chairman of the Sverdlovsk Tourist club, testified that a group of guys woke him around 7:30 A.M. to observe an unusual phenomenon in the sky; a large bright spot was observed. The phenomenon produced different impressions for different people.

Soldiers Alexandr Novikov and Alexandr Savkin also witnessed the fireball in the sky on February 17, 1959, at 6.40 A.M. They saw a bright white ball of light.

George Skoryh, a supervisor at the logging site in the village of Karaul, witnessed around mid-February 1959 between 6:00 A.M. and 7:00

A.M., a large ball of light the size of the sun or moon. He did not hear any noise from the ball.

Rescue worker N. Kouzminov witnessed fireballs in the sky in March 1959. Kouzminov and other rescue workers came to believe that the fireballs could be linked to the deaths of the Dyatlov hikers.

Local hikers and search volunteers Georgy Atmanaki and Vladimir Shavkunov spoke of seeing orbs in the sky over the northern Urals on February 17. Atmanaki's testimony to investigators stated that he and Shavkunov had woken at 6:00 A.M. to make breakfast for a group of hikers. As they were preparing the food over a fire, he saw a strange white spot in the sky that he first thought was the moon. However, it then grew in size and flew swiftly west.

The last exposure on Georgy's camera, during the Dyatlov hiking group's tragic 1959 trip, looks much like a photo of an orb. The book Dead Mountain by Donnie Eichar, page 204, has a picture of the last exposure.

Today you have a lot of professional, well respected, educated, and many other people of all walks of life, seeing things in the sky that are unexplainable. When you talk to 100 different people who saw the same object, they will give you 100 different descriptions. Along with those descriptions, they will give you 100 different guesses as to what those lights in the sky may be.

The same is true with the Dyatlov case mystery. The above are only some of the testimonies given in 1959 of the lights in the sky. And the last exposure on Georgy's camera would certainly appear that one of them took a picture of one of those orbs.

Lights of Fire

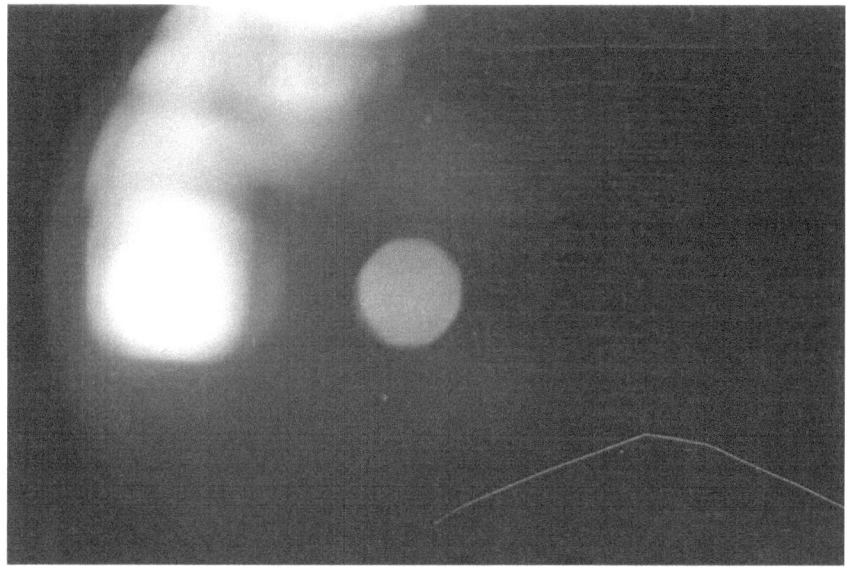

SOURCE: Krivonischenko's Camera

"And it came to pass, that as I made my journey, and was come nigh unto Damascus about noon, suddenly there shown from heaven a great light round about me. And they that were with me saw indeed the light, and were afraid; but they heard not the voice of Him that speak to me." (Acts 22: 6-9)

THE DYATLOV TRIP TO DEAD MOUNTAIN

Ten hikers, most of them were students of the Ural Polytechnic Institute (UPI), were taking a two-week cross country skiing trip in the Northern Urals. Since radios in 1959 were too heavy to carry, they were on their own during their trip and had no way to call for help once they reached the mountains. The group was provided with classified maps from the chief-in-duty of a local exploration company, and the key mountains on the hike were Otorten and Oyka-Syahl. They were expected to return to the town of Vizhai no later than February 12, 1959. This group, known as the Dyatlov Group, and another group known as the Blinov Group departed on a train north of Sverdlovsk then they were to go through Serov to the town of Ivdel and further on to Vizhai.

On January 24, 1959 they arrived in Serov at 7:00 AM. The next train was to depart in twelve hours. The Station's sitting room was locked, but Georgy Krivonischenko was inspired by the joy of companionship with friends so he started singing a song. A militia sergeant took him into custody for a few hours for disturbing the peace. People who enjoyed his good nature explained to the militia that he meant no harm, so they released him. Both groups departed Serov at 6:30 PM and arrived in Ivdel by midnight. They spent the night at the train station.

On January 25, early in the morning, both groups caught a bus to Vizhai. When they reached the village around 2:00 PM., they partied and had a good time together.

Lights of Fire

SOURCE: Krivonischenko's Camera

The Dyatlov group could not leave Vizhai with the Blinov group that day, and Lyuda wrote in her diary that the zone was closed. Sometimes their diary notes were unclear as to what they meant, but it probably meant that they were not approved to move on to the 41st site that day. They had lunch in the canteen, and some of them went and enjoyed an Italian movie called *The Gold Symphony* at the local leisure center. The tourists on duty in the group spent six hours cooking dinner on a bonfire since the wood was damp and it took some time to get the fire started. Then they all settled in for the night in a modest guest house.

On January 26, the group got up at around 9:00 AM. It was -17 degrees Celsius, and they decided not to cook on the bonfire because it took too long the night before. Lyuda was the group's purser, and she was tight with the money they spent; but on this rare occasion though, she allowed the group to eat breakfast in the village canteen. Igor arranged with the authorities for a ride on an open truck to the 41st site. They had their picture taken in the back of the truck before they left Vizhai. It was around 1:00 PM when they left Vizhai and approximately 4:30

PM when they reached the settlement at the 41st site. The locals were mostly former prisoners and men who lacked formal education, so manual labor was often their best option. They worked by contracts to harvest, chop, and haul wood from the surrounding forests. They welcomed the hikers that day and provided them with a separate room in the loggers' hotel. The tourists were impressed by the friendliness of the workers. One, nicknamed "Beard," especially impressed them with his help and kindness.

On January 27, they arranged for a horse and cart to take their backpacks from the 41st site to the 2nd northern settlement, which once served as a labor camp. During the wait for Stanislav Valyukyavichus, the driver of the horse and cart, they learned new songs from the locals. The 2nd northern settlement was 24 kilometers away; once started, the trip took them from 4:00 PM to 11:00 PM. Without the weight of their backpacks, it made the first part of the hike relaxing.

SOURCE: Wikimedia Commons

(When Yuri Yudin, the sole surviving member of the Dyatlov Group was interrogated, he told them the frazil would build up on the skis which became very daunting while travelling along the Lozva River. They would have to stop every five minutes and clean off their skis.) The settlement

sat along the Lozva River. Out of the twenty-four houses, only one had a roof, stove, and glass windows. They started a fire in the stove with boards, by which they were able to cook dinner with and it gave them a warm house to stay in. They talked till 3:00 AM before going to sleep.

On January 28, Yuri Yudin knew he had to tell the others about his back pain. From this point on, there would be no turning back; so he chose to stop there. Igor told Yuri to inform UPI that they would be gone for another two or three days. Without Yuri, they needed to spread some of his load out among themselves. The men carried backpacks weighing 40 kg, or 88 pounds. The women carried backpacks weighing 30 kg, or 66 pounds. It was before noon at the 2nd northern settlement that Yuri spoke his last words with his friends. He would go back with Stanislav, the driver of the horse-drawn cart, and will be the group's only survivor. The remaining nine hikers said their goodbyes, parting ways with him, and started traveling up along the Lozva River. Each would take turns leading in front to make the path for the others. Around 4:00 PM they stopped and stood together as they ate lunch. It was -8 Celsius, but the nearby water was seeping through the ice on the river. After a 15 kilometer hike up the river, around 5:30 PM they stopped and set up camp on the bank of the Lozva. This would be their first open-air campsite on the hike. They found a level area to place their skis as a base for the floor of the tent. After setting the tent up on top of the skis and anchoring it, they took their heavy coats off and spread them on the floor of the tent to sleep on. They put their stove together and set it in the middle of the tent. The two on duty would sleep next to it and keep it burning through the night. This was the warmest part of the tent, so they would be dressed lightly. They set their boots along the wall of the tent till they were ready to go to sleep. Some would put them under their coats to use them for pillows. Some of the hikers wore felt boots inside their ski boots and would sleep with them still on their feet. They would take out their dry clothes from their backpacks and change into them. During such hikes, the food was cooked over a bonfire if wood was available. If not, they cooked on the stove in the tent. After eating, they made notes in their diary of things that happened that day. After each person took care of their responsibility, they would settle in on their spot in the tent and cover themselves with blankets before going to sleep.

On January 29, they went from the camp along the Lozva to the camp on the Auspiya. Kolya made notes in the common diary: They followed the Mansi Trail. It was a three kilometer hike upstream to the Auspiya campsite. The weather was good, at -13 Celsius with almost no wind. They often encountered frazil on the Lozva, and that day was Yuri's (Doroshenko) birthday.

On January 30, Alexander Kolevatov and Kolya Thibault were on duty for the second time because of the slow work the previous day. It was -17 Celsius in the morning, and it took a long time to light up a bonfire. The area had Mansi writings and mysterious symbols that they didn't understand. They would follow their ski trails only to return to the river because of the struggle going through the woods. The place was beautiful with tall spruce trees and plenty of firewood for a bonfire. They ate lunch around 2:00 PM and set up camp around 5:00 PM.

On January 31, the hikers left the Auspiya River campsite around 10:00 AM. As they ascended up out of the forest, the sight of spruce and pine ended and gave way to birch trees that grew here and there. After a fourteen kilometer hike, they reached the edge of the forest. There was a strong west wind and poor visibility on the way up to the 1079 slope. When it got too steep, they went back down to the Auspiya riverbank and set up camp again. There was a lot of snow, but almost no wind when they finally found a good spot around 4:00 PM. Dyatlov noted in the group's diary that the place they reached on the slope was totally unsuitable for the overnight stay. They made plans to lighten their load and to take a more southerly route towards the Lozva Valley and then up to the north side of the slope to the 1079.

Lights of Fire

On February 1, around 10:00 AM, they made a cache for their food and things that were unnecessary for the hike and marked the place with skis. They planned to stop there on the way back, pick the things up, and finish the trip back home. The last written words from the group were the words of a humorous newspaper titled The Evening Otorten and dated February 1, 1959. Semyon Zolotaryov was good at drawing and most likely was the one who did the writing. It was probably noon when they had things packed away and were ready for the hike. A picture they took of their hike on the slope shows the low visibility. They left no records in their diaries for February 1, but it›s assumed they probably reached the 1079, the northern slope campsite, around 3:00 PM. The winds on the open slope were probably strong and made it a challenge to set the tent up. They dug out snow and leveled an area for the tent. They laid their skis down, set the tent up on top of them, and anchored it down. They went in and took their coats and boots off, lining them up along one side of the tent, and laying their coats and blankets on the floor. Someone had a napkin with slices of ham and an open flask of cocoa. These were still sitting there when searchers found the tent as if the hikers had been getting ready to start eating. It looked much like the routine described in their diary on January 28. However, something happens before they got into the routine of writing down the day's events in their diaries. The investigators know that whatever it was, it was something that made them want to get out of that tent in a hurry. The tent was cut from the inside, and the hikers left without taking their heavy coats and boots. This is the first part of the mystery that puzzles investigators. What could have happened in the tent that would make all nine hikers scramble into a harsh environment without grabbing the things needed to survive?

"Where there is no vision the people perish." (Proverbs 29:18)

OPENING THE DOOR?

Not all keys will open every door unless it is a master key. The same thing holds true with theories. Most of the theories that are out there about the Dyatlov Pass Incident do not explain the mysteries of the night. To understand a theory and to find it acceptable, we need keys that come from some ancient writings. Below and the following chapters document these writings.

Let us imagine to walk along with these nine hikers to explain the events of that night. What we want is to build a detailed hypothetical case to clarify points. One key that is required is that we give the nine hikers the respect they deserve for their experience in survival skills, and the intelligence of their professional achievements.

"Some have taken away the key of knowledge: and entered in not themselves, and them that were entering in they hindered." (Luke 11: 52)

The mistake or mistakes the hikers created were not made on that night. The theories we will discuss will be in gray boxes. Inside these gray boxes are comments on the case that may help offer insight into the mysteries. Now, to open the door to the mysteries. The following brief review with comments will now lead us into that theory.

When the nine hikers didn't return, a search party was sent out to look for them. When searchers came to the tent, they found an ice ax outside and used it to force their way in.

> Note: After the hikers cut the tent to get out, the search-and-rescue team used an ice ax to get in the tent.

The search team felt relief for a moment because there were no bodies. But as they looked around, they realized there was something very wrong with the scene. The hiking boots were lined up along the side of the tent and the coats and blankets covered the floor. A napkin with slices of ham and an open flask of cocoa sat nearby like it was waiting to be reheated. It gave the impression that the hikers may return at any moment. Their backpacks with food, money, and other items were still there. The stove sat in the middle of the tent looking as if they were about to assemble it. There was no sign of a fight or scuffle in or outside the tent. They found a trace of urine outside the tent as if somebody stepped out to relieve himself. Depending on which testimony you go by, they found the footprints of eight or nine hikers heading down the slope, one in felt boots and the rest only in socks, and one man with totally bare feet. The investigators reported the footprints to be clear and well distinguished. They said they could see the imprints of one man's toes in the snow, indicating that he was not even wearing socks while he walked to the cedar tree. The prints were adjacent and walking in a parallel chain as though the hikers were holding onto each other. It gave the appearance as if they were combing the side of the slope looking for something small. There were two groups of footprints: one larger group of about six or seven and another two pairs of footprints about 20 meters to the left heading down the slope. Then they merged again about 30 to 40 meters further down. After they merged they did not part. They walked at a normal pace disappearing temporarily on rocky strips, then showing up again as they made their way down the slope. They walked to a big cedar tree, of which the top could be seen from the tent on a clear day.

> Note: Some say these hikers made a lot of mistakes in their decisions before reaching the campsite at 1079. Some comments about the diary records with facts on the search may help to change the reasoning of them being less competent.

Dyatlov decided to leave a cache of about 55 kilograms of surplus food and gear in the Auspiya Valley, which they would have picked up on their way back home. By noon they had their non-essential things packed away and started their hike, and by 3:00 PM they reached the 1079 campsite on the slope. They had taken a picture on the way which showed poor visibility.

SOURCE: Public Domain

Note: It took the hikers about three hours from the Auspiya Valley cache site where the snow was deep, to the 1079 tent site on the slope. Their cache of food and supplies was put in a snow pit, marked with skis at the campsite. They said going to the Auspiya Valley in the first place was a mistake. It has also been suggested that when the slope became too steep, instead of going back the second time in the Auspiya Valley, if they would have gone down into the Lozva Valley and left their cache there, they may have remained alive. However, on January 30th, it was noted in the group's diary that they tried to follow a Mansi trail only to turn back to the river. And on January 31, Dyatlov noted in the group's diary about the place they reached on the slope being totally unsuitable for the overnight stay, along with the note on deep snow conditions in the Auspiya Valley. Even investigators could not get into the Lozva Valley to look for the bodies because of the depth of the snow.

Lights of Fire

> Is it possible that all the snow blew off the slope like a wind tunnel into the Lozva Valley, making the Auspiya Valley the only passable route? A lot of factors could've played a part in their decisions. Maybe with the load they were carrying, and an avalanche threat with the steep location, and the weather that could not have been foreseen, they decided to go back down and lighten their load. They needed a place where they knew they were going to be able to get to their supplies again. With it getting late in the day, they didn't want to be walking around the mountains much longer searching for a safe place to put the tent. Igor also may have wanted to look at his maps again to make sure of his plans for a safe route and a good campsite? Today the hikers' actions can be dismissed as mistakes unless one considers the limited equipment available to them in 1959. Most are now addicted to the conveniences, such as looking at their cell phones to see what the weather's going to be.

At 3:00 PM Dyatlov chose a safe avalanche free campsite where Otorten Mountain could be reached from the 1079 campsite the next day. With the wind blowing down the slope, they struggled to get the tent set up and anchored. After they were all inside the tent, it starts warming up enough that they start settling into their regular routines as described in the January 28th diary entry. Kolya Thibault had his boot liners on and steps out to relieve himself. He sees a ball of light in the night sky and steps in to tell the others. He picks up Georgy's camera and steps back out. He takes a picture of the object, and in a flash, a beam of light shoots into the tent. Like looking into a welder's arc or flashbulb, it blinds the eight hikers inside the tent. It's so bright and hot that Igor takes his knife and starts making swipes at the tent until he makes a way for them to escape. He tells them to grab what they can and follow.

> Note: When feeling intense heat, it's human nature to escape the source quickly.

Kolya Thibault sees the intense light inside the tent has blinded his friends, and that it will not let them back into the tent. Kolya tells them to join hands and follow him. Igor tells him to guide them to the cedar tree they noticed earlier in the Lozva Valley. As they were led down the slope, the hard crusted snow gives way to fluffier snow; and it melts under their feet. This forms the icy footprints which helps to preserve the prints for about a month.

> Note: Their footprints lasted longer than normal under those conditions. This circumstance would also explain the conflicting reports regarding eight or nine sets of footprints. If Kolya was the one who was outside, then the light didn't react with him; and his footprints were not preserved like the other eight hikers. The intense heat may also explain the odd skin color of some of the hikers.

Kolya has a flashlight and guides them down the slope. On the way down, something grabs hold of Zina Kolmogorova and carried her up the slope away from the others. She is thrown to the ground, which knocks the wind out of her so that she can't call out for help. Her face gets cut up by the hard crusted snow and the brutal attack. She struggles to get up, but there's a force that holds her down. Her fingers become frostbitten, but she knows if she gives up, she will freeze to death in the brutal cold temperatures. The terrifying struggle finally takes its toll, and she grows tired and she falls into an exhausted sleep.

> Note: Questions were asked about why Zina's pants were undone and her blouse unbuttoned. With all the hikers inside the tent, it starts warming up enough to start changing into dry clothes. The hikers were probably in the middle of their routine when they were visited, and she didn't have time to button back up. Being the one found closest to the tent, it would only seem like Zina was trying to return to the tent.

Zina was the third to the last in the chain going down the slope. The last two blind hikers had no idea what happened to her, and they ended up walking twenty meters to the left of the other hikers. They called out and are able to get back to them again with the help of Kolya's flashlight. Once they reached the cedar tree, Igor finds out that Zina was no longer with them. The two hikers who had been holding her hand explain to

Igor that they lost her grip somehow on the way down, and they didn't know what happened to her. They are starting to get their eyesight back by this time, so they get a fire going underneath the cedar tree. Igor does not want to lose anyone else, so he instructs Georgy Krivonischenko and Yuri Doroshenko to keep the fire going under the cedar tree. He told the other five hikers to start working on making a floor down in the ravine out of the wind. He told them to make sure they can still see the light from the fire under the tree, and stay together. Making a floor would be hard work, and it would take everybody doing their share to survive this very cold, dark night. The Five hikers were Lyuda Dubinina, Alexander Kolevatov, Kolya Thibault, Semyon Zolotaryov, and Rustik Slobodin. They cut down some fir trees and drag them into the ravine. The light of the fire helps them to see, and the snow was not as deep, so it made it easier to accomplish the work for the floor. Igor told them he was going back up the slope to find Zina. He tells them to keep the fire burning so that Zina may see it, and being without a flashlight the light will help to guide himself back. He had no idea what danger was awaiting him up the slope. He only knew he wasn't going to let Zina be stranded alone. On his way back up to find Zina, he sees something coming toward him. As the night visitor swing at his head, he raises his left hand to block the blow; but it still knocked him unconscious. He lay face down in the snow still breathing. He never awakes again from this unconscious sleep and he passes away from hypothermia. Yuri and Georgy, being down at the fire, didn't see what happened to Igor. The floor was about finished, so Rustem tells the other four hikers he is going to go back up to see how the search for Zina was going. When he got there Yuri and Georgy told him they hadn't heard or seen anything yet. Rustem tells them he's going to go see if he could help Igor find Zina. He says to them when it becomes hard to see the light from the fire, he would turn right back. He gives them the signals he will use with the flashlight if he finds them, so Yuri climbs up the cedar tree to get a better view up the slope. Rustem reached the place where Igor was face down in the snow. He turned him over, and found the cold wind-chill temperature has frozen Igor's body stiff. Rustem signals with his flashlight that he found Igor. He can still see the light of the fire, so he continued up the slope and shouts out for Zina. About halfway between Igor and Zina, Rustem sees a ghost-like figure moving toward him. Before he can run, it knocks the flashlight out of his hand and picks him up off the ground by his head. The force is so great that it cracks his skull and disfigures his head. Yuri can hear the faint sound of Rustem's horrific scream being carried along with the winds down the slope. Then, with a burst of light, Rustem falls back to the ground. The heat of his body melts the snow more than five centimeters.

> Note: It was noted that Rustem's leg was tucked up underneath him, but his body was still able to melt the snow which re-froze into ice over five centimeters deep. This burst of light reacting with Rustem's body would explain that much ice under him on such a cold night.

Yuri saw the night visitor and what just happened to Rustem. He then watched the visitor as it dimmed again into a ghost-like figure which started to move toward the Cedar tree. In his panicked haste to warn the others, Yuri fell to the ground, breaking limbs on the way down. He tells Georgy what he just saw, and shouts down to the others as quiet as he can that there was some kind of beast coming. With everything that has happened so far, they had no reason to doubt the panic-stricken warning that there was something dangerous on the way. Georgy and Yuri with haste try to hide the light of the fire by falling over it.

> Note: Experts give biological reasons for people falling into the fire when they are freezing, but it seems a little unlikely that this symptom would happen to two people at the same time without one hiker being able to help the other. Also, as to the voices being able to carrying to the floor which was 50 meters from the cedar tree, searchers said they could hear people talk at the cedar tree while they stood at the floor.

As the fire burns through what clothes they have on, the ghost-like figure closes in on top of them and held them down so that they couldn't

Lights of Fire

move. This smothered the fire; and like Zina, after some time they grew into an exhausted sleep and froze to death.

> Note: It would seem like the brutal visitor, used the first hikers as bait to lure the others to help them. This scenario also shows the visitors enjoyment of the irony of people getting severely burned while freezing to death.

After not hearing anything from Georgy and Yuri for a long time, Alexander told the other three hikers to wait at the floor while he went to the cedar tree to see what was going on. Alexander finds Yuri and Georgy overcome by hypothermia, so he tried to take as much clothing and supplies like matches, that he thinks they would need to survive the night. He returned with the clothes and divided them out amongst the other three. They used some of the clothes to set in and covered themselves the best they could. Alexander then told them what he saw at the cedar tree. Semyon Zolotaryov pulls his diary and pencil out of his jacket pocket to record some of the events of that night along with what Alexander just told him. It was close to 3:00 AM by then; and before he can write anything down, the ghost-like figure approaches them. The valley was filled by light from the night visitor as it grabbed Lyuda, crushing her chest cavity and breaking ribs on both sides. It pulls her head up to its mouth and spews acid into her mouth. And just like a scorpion, it sucked her tongue out, taking her lower teeth and upper lip with it, leaving an unusual mobility in the neck area. Its laser-like eyes burned her eyes out, completely blinding her. And like a scorpion, it literally sucked the life out of her. It tossed her like a rag doll to a nearby frozen stream six meters away.

> Note: The investigators believe the stream was frozen solid that time of year. They also figure she had about ten minutes after the chest injury to live. When investigator Lev Ivanov, opens Lyuda's coffin to show her father that his daughter was dressed properly, he was so horrified by the sight of her that he fainted on the spot. Documentation of why the night visitor may have mimicked the scorpion with Lyuda will be covered in a later chapter.

The visitor picked Kolya Thibault up by his head and shoulder, giving him a 17-centimeter long crack at the base of the skull, a bone fracture on the right side of his skull, with the temporal bone bulged into the cranial cavity. He too was cast to the frozen stream like a rag doll. The injury didn't kill him right away, but he still lay there on the frozen stream in shock. Alexander Kolevatov, like the other three hikers, was paralyzed with fear when they saw what happened to Lyuda. Knowing it was his turn, as soon as the night visitor picked up his terror-stricken body, he had a heart attack. He was also tossed like a rag doll to the frozen stream. Semyon Zolotaryov had a diary in one hand and a pencil in the other hand, when the visitor came into the ravine. Being in shock, he too provided little resistance when the visitor picked him up by the chest, fracturing his ribs. Having been paralyzed by his fear and pain, Semyon's hands held on tight to the pencil and diary as he was tossed like a rag doll to the frozen stream.

Source: Russian National Archives

The bodies of Kolevatov, Zolotarev and Thibault-Brignoles

> Note: All of the hikers at the creek who didn't immediately die of their injuries were not going to move from this final resting place due to shock. Alexander having a heart attack because of this horrifying experience would be the only reason he would stay laying there next to his three friends that had the bone crushing injuries.

About 3:00 AM this horrifying struggle for life came to an end.

> Note: Comments made by people that have seen evil events, notice that signs from evil show up at 3:00 A.M. It's the opposite of 3:00 PM, when the Spirit of Christ departed His body, and the darkness lifted from off the earth. (**See Reference:** Matthew 27: 45-50) This theory walked through the night with the nine hikers, explaining the mysteries surrounding the case as much as possible. The following chapters will document similar stories of night visitors from thousands of years ago. This chapter started with a man guiding blind hikers into a dark ravine. It would only be fitting to end the chapter with a written story of a man guiding blind soldiers to the understanding of the Light of the world.

About 900 B.C., a Syrian king was looking for a prophet named Elisha. Elisha was telling the king of Israel all the secrets of the Syrian king, by the hand of the Lord above. So the king sent a large number of soldiers with horses and chariots after Elisha. When Elisha's servant woke early in the morning, he saw the city was encompassed with this great number of soldiers, horses, and chariots. Elisha's servant told him they were finished. Elisha answered him saying, he was not to fear; he said there's more with us than there are with them. His servant could not believe what he was hearing from Elisha; So Elisha prayed and asked the Lord to open his servant's eyes that he may see. So, the Lord opened his eyes and the servant saw the mountains were full of horses and chariots of fire. Then Elisha prayed unto the Lord again and asked Him to strike the Syrian army with blindness. And the Lord struck the Syrian army with blindness. Then Elisha told the Syrian army to follow him; so the Syrian army, being blind, followed Elisha hand in hand to Samaria. Then he asked the Lord to open their eyes, and the

Lord opened their eyes; and they saw that they were in Samaria in the midst of the Israelites. The king of Israel asked about destroying them, and Elisha said no. So, they left the Syrian army go back to the king of Syria, not to be bothered by that king of Syria again. They were blinded, and then their eyes were opened to the enlightenment of the powers, and the kindness of the living God. (*See reference:* 2 King 6:11-23)

"I, the lord, have called you in righteousness, and will hold your hand... And give you for a light.... To open the blind eyes...." (Isaiah 42: 6-7)

"And if the blind lead the blind, both shall fall into the ditch." (Matthew 15:14)

"Who is confident that you yourself are a guide of the blind, a light of them which are in darkness?" (Romans 2:19)

The Soviet Empire was a very dark, oppressive, and dominating Empire. The hikers were working to help that Empire with the nuclear weapons which were created to destroy the Lord's people who live in freedom. Yuri Yudin was spared the fate of the other nine hikers so he could ask that faithful question. "If I could ask God just one question it would be what really happened to my friends that night?" -Yuri Yudin (1937-2013)

"I will give unto you the keys of the Kingdom of heaven." (Matthew 16:19)

"After this I looked, and behold, a door was opened in heaven: and I heard a voice say, 'come up here, and I will show you things which must come hereafter.'" (Revelations 4:1)

BRIEF HISTORY OF BIBLE AND STRONG'S DICTIONARY

This chapter will briefly cover the history of the Bible, and a valuable dictionary for looking into the languages of the Bible. Both books will document the theory, which will be shown later.

In 1959 there were reports of lights in the sky that surrounded the story of the Dyatlov Pass incident. These lights, orbs, lamps, or fireballs, whatever you want to call them, surrounded another incident. The lights in the sky around these incidents has a connection to some unbelievable answers. But just because people will not believe a thing doesn't mean it's not real! Scientists deal with unbelievable things every day. But scientists will take those unbelievable things, they will search for the answers, and find why it can be believed. Those answers must fit like a key going into a door lock, otherwise they don't have the right key or answer for understanding. Much like the theories discussed behind the Dyatlov Pass Incident do not fit the signs of that night. They do not bring forth the key that opens the door of understanding nor provide the answers for all those mysteries. They say as time passes, people start making things out of things that did not happen or make things up that were not there. The theory that was given in this book is based as much as possible on everything that has been documented or written. Considering some things were compromised by the search team in the beginning and conflicting reports of the investigation, it was intended to stay only with what they documented. One of things around the event that does not conflict is the lights in the sky. There is only conflicting views as to what they were. The documentation requires going back approximately 3,000 years into these writings and stories of supernatural events. The Dyatlov Pass Incident was a big enough mystery that they opened the case again sixty years later. Anyone who looked into the signs around that event cannot get around the fact that there were things that could not be explained by the forces of nature. The case was closed with the words, "An Unknown Compelling Force". Investigators could not begin to give the hikers' families the key of understanding as to what compelled them to do those things.

The following shares some history and facts for those that care to be acquainted with the sources, information, and documentation used for the theory. If this is not your interest, you can skim over, or move on to the next chapter, if you like.

In the year 1611, a book came into existence by the order of a king. That king's name is King James, the person responsible for the King James Version of the Bible; produced from the first order given for the translation of the Hebrew and Greek Manuscripts into English. This English version of these Manuscripts translated into the K.J.V. Bible has a concordance that takes each word, where it's found, and has a dictionary for that word. The Old Testament is mostly from the Hebrew Manuscripts, with some Aramaic; and the New Testament is from the Greek. Without going into a lot of detail, the Strong's Exhaustive Concordance (see Figure 1 below) is a good work that has a dictionary for the Hebrew and Greek languages (see Figures 2 and 3 below).

Figure 1: Front Cover of the Strong's Exhaustive Concordance of the Bible

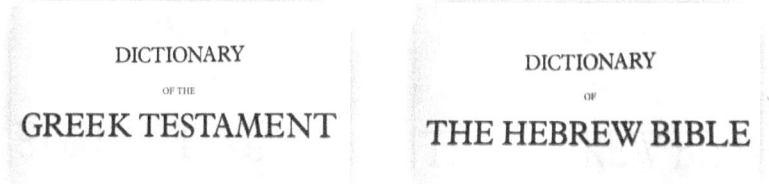

Figure 2 and 3: Hebrew and Greek Dictionaries found in the Strong's Exhaustive Concordance of the Bible

Every word found in the King James Version Bible will be found alphabetically in the Strong's Concordance, the same as a regular dictionary. Under the word that you're looking for there will be a list of sentences with only the first letter of that word in the sentence. After each sentence you will find where that word can be found in the King James Bible, and the number that will take you to the definition of the Hebrew word in the Hebrew dictionary, if it is from the Old Testament.

If the word is in the New Testament, you will find the definition by going to the Greek dictionary with the number that is given. In the back of the Strong's Concordance you will find the Hebrew and Greek dictionary. The Hebrew dictionary is numbered from 1 to 8674. After each number it will show how the Hebrew word looks in the Manuscripts, then how to pronounce it, and then the meaning. This is the same way with words in the New Testament and the Greek dictionary being numbered from 1 to 5624. The Strong's Concordance actually gives you a copy of the Manuscripts, again by showing the words appearance in the languages, with a pronunciation of them, along with the meaning (see Figure 4). In some cases, you will see that the word in the Manuscripts was translated over into different English words.

An example will be shown here which will deal with the theory.

```
OREB (o'-reb)
    1. A prince of Midian.
  two princes of the Midianites, O............ Judg 7:25   6157
  they slew O upon the rock O, ................ Judg 7:25   6157
  Midian, and brought the heads of O..... Judg 7:25   6157
  hands the princes of Midian, O .............. Judg 8:3    6157
  Make their nobles like O, and like ........ Ps 83:11     6157
```

Figure 4: The word "OREB" found in the Strong's Exhaustive Concordance

Before getting to the definition of the name Oreb, there is a video you may find interesting posted by William Guy, on September 28, 2019. The video of 14 balls of light, hovering silently out over the ocean. The video was taken during a ferry boat ride across the Pimlico Sound, North Carolina. The balls of light are hovering like swarms of mosquitoes, which should help with the visualization of the definition, and the understanding of Oreb's name.

In this example the Hebrew dictionary numbers 6157 and 6148 (see Figures 5a, 5b and 6 below).

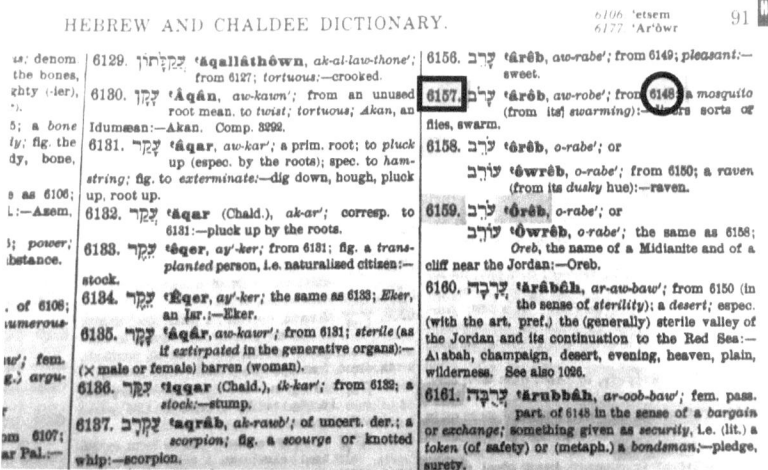

Figure 5a: The word "Oreb" on the Hebrew and Chaldee Dictionary also references 6148

6157. עָרֹב **ʻârôb,** *aw-robe'*; from **6148**; a *mosquito* (from its *swarming*):—**divers sorts of flies, swarm.**

Figure 5b: The meaning of Oreb on 6157

6148. עָרַב **ʻârab,** *aw-rab'*; a prim. root; to *braid*, i.e. *intermix*; techn. to *traffic* (as if by barter); also to *give* or *be security* (as a kind of exchange):—**engage, (inter-) meddle (with), mingle (self), mortgage, occupy, give pledges, be (-come, put in) surety, undertake.**

Figure 6: The meaning of the "Oreb" on 6148

The back portion of the Strong's Concordance will be marked at the top of the pages for the languages of the dictionary. Chaldee, and Aramaic, is the same language, which covers about 70 years of the Israelites history, in which the 70-year period falls in the Old Testament. After

Israel came out of Babylon, the language changed to Greek which the four Gospels, the Epistles, and the book of Revelation are written. On the previous page shows the Hebrew dictionary with the definition of the word Oreb. The word orb does not appear in the King James Bible, but Oreb comes close to the word orb, which ties the two words together with the Isaiah 10: 26 reference to lamps, and the prime root definition. The theory of angels intermixing, mingling themselves, and engaging to braid themselves in among the humans on earth.

There are other very good tools also, but this is enough detail of how the Manuscripts can be researched. Again, a Bible is only as good as the man who translated it. Today you have a lot of translations of the Manuscripts into English; but when you use most of them, you have no way of verifying that person's translation. So you need a King James Bible if you want to go back into the languages. The Strong's Concordance is a good tool for checking things out for yourself. When going through these stories and documentations for the theory, the references will be next to that statement. Some translations are so poorly done, that you will never be able to reference anything from them! The references given in this book will be strictly from the King James version and will document the theory and the thoughts behind the reference. You may find that it is not word for word reference, (paraphrasing), but the thought will be found therein those references. Like all theories, everybody can make their own mind up if the key fits the facts.

"If you seek it as silver, and search for it as hidden treasures; Then you shall understand the fear of the Lord, and find the knowledge of God. For the Lord gives wisdom: Out of His mouth, comes knowledge and understanding." (Proverbs 2: 4- 6)

"Take heed to yourself: behold, I have foretold you all things." (Mark 13:23)

"The same anointing teaches you of all things, and is truth, and is no lie." (1 John 2:27)

"At midnight there was a cry made. Give us of your oil; for our lamps are going out. And the door was shut." (Matt 25: 6- 10)

"According to the slaughter of Midian at the rock of Oreb:" (Isaiah 10: 26)

"Because of the anointing…" Oil of Gideon's lamps. (Isaiah 10:27)

GIDEON'S LAMPS

Our Creator of the heavens and the earth, along with Gideon's lamps will shine some light on a supernatural slaughter.

About the year 1225 BC, there was a man named Gideon. Gideon was of the family of Manasseh which is a tribe of Israel. He was a poor man without much recognition among his people. *(See reference:* Judges 6:15) The Creator of the heavens and the earth heard the cries of the children of Israel about how the Midianites and the people of the east were destroying them. This destruction came because they had been doing evil in the Lord's sight, so He withdrew Himself from Israel and left the Midianites to oppress them for seven years. *(See reference:* Judges 6:1-2)

> Like always, the evil starts with the breaking of His Commandments. Adultery, coveting, stealing, and killing each other. This all comes along with pushing Him out of our lives, and not thanking Him for our blessings. Just like today, the morals have gone out the window, and the next thing murders run rampant. There's nothing new under the sun. He does not miss a thing! No mysteries!

Then comes the influx of other people to eat up Israel's substance. *(See reference: Judges 6:4)* So when the oppression came to the point when they cried out to the Lord for help, He came and met with Gideon. Gideon was by the winepress threshing wheat because he was trying to hide it from those that wanted to take it for free. *(See reference: Judges 6:11)*

> The mindset of mixed multitudes is that you can take things for free. Margaret Thatcher said socialism works very well until you run out of other people's substance. Why work when you can show up and get things for free that other people worked for? The Creator does not like those that take things by force just because they can. He allows it to happen to teach His people a lesson. The lesson not to covet the rich man, which always, always leads to murder, and worse! As we go through the supernatural slaughters keep in mind why they happen.

"Gideon said unto to the Lord if the Lord be with us then why is all this happening to us? Did not the Lord bring us up out of the land of Egypt? And now the Lord has forsaken us and delivered us into the hand of the Midianites. Where are all the Lord's miracles which our fathers told us about?" (Judges 6:13)

> The obvious answer to that question was that they forsook Him and His Commandments. Thou shall not covet the system of socialism. Evil things spring forth from socialism, like murders, and oppression. Look around today at all the shootings, and people working harder to support socialism. There is nothing new under the sun.

The Lord told Gideon that He was going to use him to deliver Israel from the Midianites. Gideon, being a poor man without much recognition, didn't know how that could be. Gideon was not sure who he was talking to, and he asked the Angel of the Lord to wait until he went and got some meat and unleavened cakes. When he came back, the Angel of the Lord told him to set it on the rock; and the Angel of the Lord put forth His staff and touched the flesh and the unleavened cakes. There rose fire out of the rock and consumed the flesh and the unleavened cakes. Then the Angel of the Lord disappeared out of his sight. Gideon was now sure who he was talking to; and since he saw the Lord, he thought he was going to die. And the Lord spoke and told him to fear not. (See reference: Judges 6: 17-24)

> A few supernatural things happened there to strengthen Gideon's faith.

Lights of Fire

Gideon had gathered men together to go up against Midian. And the Lord told him that he had too many men with him. He had 32,000 men and he told them whoever had fear about going to war could return. 22,000 people return home and 10,000 remained. And the Lord told him there are still too many people with you. After eliminating the men through a series of tests, he ended up with 300 men to go against Midian. (See reference: Judges 7: 2- 7)

> This was done so that the men of Israel would not become prideful and think they were the ones who defeated the Midianites.

The Midianites were in the valley beneath Gideon, and they were like grasshoppers for a multitude of 135,000. (See references: Judges 7:12 and Judges 8:10)

> Now we have 300 men going against 135,000 men.

The Lord knew that Gideon was going to need a confidence boost. So He told Gideon to take another man with him and go down into the valley and listen in on the Midianites. When Gideon got down there, he heard a soldier tell another soldier about a dream that he had. He said he dreamed a dream, and he saw a barley cake tumble into the host of Midian and it came to a tent and hit so that it fell. Another soldier answered back and said, this is the sword of Gideon, for God has delivered the host of Midian into his hand. When Gideon heard the dream and the interpretation of the dream, he worshiped the Lord and returned to the 300 men. (See reference: Judges 7: 9- 15)

> Gideon knew that the Lord had to be responsible for this dream. After hearing the dream and the interpretation, the first thing he did was to worship the Lord. This means he acknowledged the Lord and gave Him thanks.

"Let us offer the sacrifice of praise to God continually, that is the fruit of our lips giving thanks to His Name." (Hebrews 13:15)

"The Lord said, Israel is my son, even my firstborn." (Exodus 4:22)

> Barley bread is the first grain to be harvested for bread. Wheat and barley being the good seed which is symbolic of His people. (*See references:* Matthew 13: 24-30 + 36-41) These references are where the interpretation of the dream comes from, but this was made known to the Midianite soldiers. They also heard about the Lord bringing Israel up out of the land of Egypt.

"Woe unto us! who shall deliver us out of the hand of these mighty gods? These are the Gods that inflicted and destroyed Egypt with all the plagues in the wilderness." (1 Samuel 4:8)

> Like we hear the story about Columbus discovering America in 1492 A.D. All the nations heard about the plague of angels on the Egyptians, which made a bigger impact than Columbus discovering America.

Gideon was told to take the 300 men and divide them into three companies on every side of the Midianite camp. Each man was to take a trumpet, empty picture, and a lamp. They were instructed to cover the lamp with the pitcher until the middle watch, which is midnight. At midnight they were told to blow the trumpet and break the pitchers that covered the lamps. So when midnight came, they blew the trumpets and broke the pitchers and cried the words, the sword of the Lord and of Gideon. (*See reference:* Judges 7:15-20)

> This is very important for understanding the 1959 hiking event! The Lord was getting ready to break the yoke of oppression that the Midianites had on Israel.

"Because of the anointing." (Isaiah 10:27)

> Connecting the two supernatural slaughters.

"After the manner of Egypt." (Isaiah 10:26)

"The Lord cast upon them the fierceness of His anger, Wrath, and Indignation, and trouble, by sending evil angels among them." (Psalms 78:49)

Lights of Fire

"And He killed all the firstborn in Egypt." (Psalm 78: 51)

"At midnight there was a cry." (Exodus 12: 29- 30 + Judges 7: 19- 21)

Which ties in with the lamps and the cry at midnight in Matthew 25: 6- 8.

> And now we have the oil in the lamps of Gideon. The midnight cry in Egypt will be covered in a later chapter.

The Midianites came and stood around the camp, and then they all cried and fled. And the Lord set every man's sword against his fellow man, even all through the host. (*See reference:* Judges 7: 21-22)

> So what just happened there? We are not given specific details as to why the Midianite army started killing each other. Our Creators Word is a fantastic jigsaw puzzle that needs to be put together to see the full picture. So what pieces of the puzzle do we have? 1. The prince of Midian whose name was Oreb has the Strong's Concordance number 6148, which gives the prime root meaning as the intermixing, mingling, and 'to braid'. (This Strong's Dictionary was covered in the last chapter.) 2. There was a scourge after the manner of Egypt, in which evil angels killed the first born of the houses without the blood on the doorposts. 3. The Midianites knew by the dream, and the interpretation of it, that the God of Israel was going to deliver the host of Midian into the hands of Gideon. 4. What was the purpose of the lamps at the top of the mountain? Presenting a theory. A. They heard the stories of the Evil angels in Egypt. B. The Army of Midian had an experience like the Dyatlov Pass experience. C. Then they receive the dream and the interpretation of it. D. The same stories of the lights in the sky, with an intermixing angel, spread through the camp and scares the Midianites out of their minds. F. At midnight they hear the trumpets and they come out and look at the lamps or balls of fire that appear to be coming over the mountains, in the sky. G. Our Creator Himself starts a chain reaction.

They think these angels are intermixing among themselves, and they start killing each other thinking that they are angels. It's just a theory, but the Soviet Union stopped the hikes from going to the Ural

Mountains for three years. In 1973, near Mt. Alaktic in Yakutia, a group of geologists died equally as mysteriously. Without any signs of violent death, their bodies were later found two kilometers away from their hastily abandoned tent. All were lightly dressed, some even without boots—so similar! Only then [in 1973], people fled in all directions, each to his side. *Dyatlov pass Keeps Its Secret* {Page 54}, is a case more like the Gideon case around 1225 BC.

Conclusion of the slaughter of Oreb.

The Midians must have known that the fallen angels can intermix, mingle, and braid themselves among the troops undetected. The trumpets blow at midnight and they go out and look up at the lamps at the mountain tops, and the Lord Himself starts a chain reaction among them. Before you know it they are all slaughtering themselves because of the wild stories of the evil angels. And seeing the lamps at the mountain tops made them think they were seeing the orbs in connection with the evil angels. The 300 men at the top of the mountains have no room for pride for the defeat of 135,000 Midianites. They know the truth and what happened to cause such fear. They know it's a fearful thing to fall into the hands of the living God. After all, they spent seven years under the yoke of the Midian oppression. (*See reference:* Judges 7:16-25)

Knowing that there is nothing new under the sun, the nine Russian hikers helped with the understanding of the theory on the slaughter of the Midianites. The four pieces of the puzzle start to show a pretty good picture. Would that not be the logical reason the Midianites started killing each other?

The 300 men of Gideon overtook two leaders of Midian, Oreb, and Zeeb. They killed Oreb at the rock of Oreb, and Zeeb they killed at the winepress. (*See reference:* Judges 7:25)

Sometimes names are given in His Word for a reason.

1. The name Immanuel or Emmanuel = God is with us

"Therefore, the Lord Himself shall give you a sign; behold, a virgin shall conceive, and bear a Son, and shall call His name Immanuel." (Isaiah 7: 14)

"Immanuel" (Isaiah 8: 8)

"For God is with us." (Isaiah 8: 10)

"Emmanuel which being interpreted is God with us." (Matthew 1: 23)

2. The name Cyrus = The rising of the sun

"Thus saith the Lord to his anointed, to Cyrus." (Isaiah 45: 1)

"That they may know from the rising of the sun." (Isaiah 45: 6)

"I have raised him up in righteousness." (Isaiah 45: 13)

3. The name Abraham = Father of a multitude or Father of many nations

"Neither shall thy name any more be called Abram, but thy name shall be called Abraham; for a father of many nations have I made thee." (Genesis 17: 5)

Names have a meaning and they give a message to the reader.

Other takeaways from the story of Gideon.

The oppression made Gideon hide at a winepress. (*See reference:* Judges 6: 11)

Zeeb was slaughtered at a winepress. (*See reference:* Judges 7: 25)

There's another slaughter coming at a winepress. (*See reference:* Revelation 14:19-20)

"For everyone one from the least even unto the greatest is given to covetousness." (Jeremiah 8: 10)

Knowing this helps us to stay on guard with trying not to covet what others have. When we look around today, we see how socialism and its oppressions, causes people to work harder to support all the coveting, which leads to shootings, and other destructive behaviors.

Dead Mountain, by Donnie Eichar, speaks of the oppression in Russia. He talks about a rock they call boot rock which he has a picture of in his book. Like most rocks with a name, it stands out. Probably like the rock of Oreb. It is ironic about the rock being called boot rock. There also is a picture taken by one of the nine Russian hikers which looks much like an orb. It's the last exposure taken with Georgy's camera in 1959.

The Lamps with Anointing Oil and Gideon's Lamps.

"At midnight there was a cry made. And the foolish said unto the wise, give us of your oil for our lamps are going out." (Matthew 25: 6- 8)

At midnight they cried and said, the sword of the Lord, and of Gideon. (*See reference:* Judges 7: 19- 20)

"Because of the anointing." (Isaiah 10: 27)

"But you have an unction from the Holy One, and you know all things." (1 John 2: 20)

"The same anointing teaches you of all things, and is truth, and is no lie." (1 John 2: 27)

To sum it up: The anointing that comes from the Holy One will light your lamp with the oil of His truth!

PASSOVER / AFTER THE MANNER OF EGYPT

Joseph was chosen to save the Lord's children from a great famine by preserving them in the land of Egypt. (*See reference:* Genesis 45: 5-7) A Pharaoh came along hundreds of years later who did not know Joseph, and the children of Israel started to multiply greatly. This new Pharaoh of Egypt was afraid that they would join their enemies and leave the land of Egypt. So the Pharaoh came up with the idea of putting taskmasters over the children of Israel to afflict them with heavy burdens. They made their lives bitter with hard bondage, in mortar, and in brick, and in all manner of services in the field: they made them serve with rigor. (*See reference:* Exodus 1: 7-14)

> The hard bondage of Egypt did not happen for no reason to the people of Israel. They have not been out of the land of Egypt very long before they started making other gods to serve. (*See reference:* Exodus 32: 1-6) This did not spring up overnight after being delivered from Egypt. Being that there's nothing new under the sun, look at how many are under hard bondage in America because of the sticks of their car payments, and bricks of their house mortgage. How many covet socialism, the very system that puts people under hard bondage? People start trusting and serving the socialism of man for their protection and needs and forget trusting in the Lord for help. They have no time for our Heavenly Father. When reading about these people after they came out of Egypt, take a good look around today. There is nothing new under the sun. (Ecclesiastes 1: 9).

The Pharaoh instructed the midwives Shiphrah and Puah, to kill the firstborn sons of the children of Israel. (*See reference:* Exodus 1:15-22)

> Shiphrah and Puah were two God-fearing women who did the delivery of the Hebrew babies. They would not kill the sons of Israel for obvious reasons! They feared our Creator more than the Pharaoh of Egypt. These two God-fearing women were part of a remnant, the same as the wise men who came and worshiped a baby because they saw His Star. They knew and trusted the Lord.

"Thus saith the Lord, Israel is my son, even my firstborn." (Exodus 4:22)

"Even so at this present time also there is a remnant according to the election of grace." (Romans 11:5)

"Behold, there came wise men from the East to Jerusalem, to worship Emmanuel." (Matt 2:1- 2)

> The Wise knew the first commandment of not having any other gods of worship. (*See reference:* Exodus 20:2) The two women knew not to touch the Lord's first born. The remnant knows our Creator, and know not to harm His people. The Pharaoh will learn this the hard way.

"In the beginning was the Word, and the Word was with God, and the Word was God." (John 1: 1)

Another God-fearing woman gave birth to Moses, and she put him in a basket to save him from the murderers in Egypt. She then put him in the river so that an Egyptian woman would come along and love this little boy, and save his life. When the daughter of the pharaoh saw him, she couldn't help but love him. Moses's sister, Miriam, approached and asked the daughter of Pharaoh if she needed the boy nursed for her. The Pharaoh's daughter said yes, and she paid Moses's mother for doing this. (*See reference:* Exodus 2: 1- 10). By faith, Moses's parents hid him for three months; and they were not afraid of the king's commandment to kill him. (*See reference:* Hebrews 11: 23) When Moses was grown, he went to visit his people; and he saw an Egyptian hitting one of his brethren under his burden. Moses looked around to make sure there were no other Egyptians, then he killed the Egyptian and hid him in the sand. Moses went out again and saw two of his people fighting amongst themselves.

Lights of Fire

Moses said to the one who did the wrong that he shouldn't do this thing. The man who did the wrong said, who made you a judge over us? Do you intend to kill me like you killed the Egyptian? When this got back to the Pharaoh, he sought to kill Moses, and Moses had to flee Egypt. (*See reference:* Exodus 2: 11- 15)

> Our Creator heard the cries from the children of Israel. The Lord needed to use Moses to deliver His people from that bondage. The way Moses killed the Egyptian will be used to make a point in "The Four Horns of Slaughter". The difference between murder and kill will be made clear with this case and with some other examples. This part of it will be known now. Moses killed the Egyptian! Moses did not murder the Egyptian! The Egyptian would've killed Moses' brother by working him like that. The Egyptians were working the people of Israel to death, so they could keep the population under Pharaoh's control. (*See reference:* Exodus 1: 9- 13)

"Moses chose to suffer the affliction with the people of God, rather than to enjoy the pleasures of sin for a season." (Hebrews 11:25)

"...these things happened for an example." (1 Corinthians 10:11)

Moses went to the backside of the desert to Horeb where the Angel of Lord spoke to him. He spoke to him out of a flame of fire in the midst of a bush. When Moses saw it, he stepped a little closer to see what he was seeing. The bush was engulfed in flames, but it was not being consumed. (*See reference:* Exodus 3: 1- 3)

> He could see that this fire was different from the ordinary fire that we know. Probably like there's more than one kind of clear liquid. One clear liquid you can drink while another clear liquid can kill you. It's hard to understand things of this nature, but the fire was maybe in another dimension? In the case of Aaron's two sons, it was able to consume them. (*See reference:* Leviticus 10: 1-2) Aaron's two sons offered strange fire. The fire in this dimension may be called strange because it's not pure? This example is another warning for those who teach our Creator's Word. Do not play with fire.

"For our God is a consuming fire." (Hebrews 12:29)

"Is not My Word like as a fire?" (Jeremiah 23:29)

"His Name is called the Word of God." (Revelation 19: 13)

> He doesn't want His children hurt by false doctrines in His Name!

The Lord told Moses that He is going to use him to set His people free. Then Moses went and told the Pharaoh that the Lord wanted His people to go on a three days' journey into the wilderness to worship Him. (*See reference:* Exodus 5: 1- 3) Pharaoh said, "who is the Lord that I should obey His voice to let Israel go? I know nothing of the Lord neither will I let Israel go." (Exodus 5:2) "Let there be more work laid upon the men that they may labor therein, and let them not regard vain words." (Exodus 5:9)

> "Vain Words, who is the Lord, and I will not obey His Voice." Very arrogant and oppressive people are willingly ignorant to mock our Father. Our Heavenly Father did give him a chance with the three-day journey option to no avail.

The Pharaoh laid more work unto the children of Israel. When the elders of Israel saw Moses and Aaron, they said, "you didn't help us a bit, and now the Egyptians look to put more work on us, and slay us with the sword." Then Moses went back and asked the Lord about it. (*See reference:* Exodus 5: 11-23)

> We are getting to the place of the Passover. But after the Hebrews are out of Egypt, they will desire again for the things in Egypt. They will forget about the things they whined about, and how the king of Egypt was trying to keep them under his thumb with rigorous work. Most people don't bother with the Lord until they want something. And after He blesses them, they rarely give Him a thank you or remember His help.

There were ten lepers whom Christ healed as they were on their way to see the priest, as Christ instructed. Out of the ten healed on the way, only one returned and glorified God and gave thanks. (*See reference:* Luke 17:12-18)

> It doesn't go unnoticed by our Creator, any more than when we do something for somebody, and they walk away without giving us a thank you. After the Pharaoh started killing the Lord's firstborn, the Pharaoh bet everything in Egypt that he could win against the Creator.

The waters became blood; infestations of frogs, lice, and flies came; hail amidst fire mingled and rained down on them; locusts destroyed crops; thick darkness that could be felt...covered them; and then, the Passover comes. *(See reference:* Exodus 7: 17- 10: 23) God's people were instructed to take a lamb without blemish and prepare it for the Passover. Each person in each house was to have enough to eat. The blood was to go on the lentil and the two doorposts. *(See reference:* Exodus 12:21-22) They were instructed to eat unleavened bread for seven days, from the 14th day to the 21st first day in the first month. The Passover would begin on the 14th day of the first month. The first month of the year was the month of Abib. *(See reference:* Exodus 12:8-17) They were instructed not to go out of their houses until morning, so the destroyer could not touch the people who had blood on the doorposts. *(See reference:* Exodus 12: 1-24)

> The first month of the year starts at the Spring equinox when everything comes to life. Later Solomon's temple was designed to mark the equinox which started the year by the sun shining into the Holy Temple.

"We are the children of light, and the children of the day: we are not of the night, nor of darkness." (1 Thessalonians 5:5)

> The Passover is set by the light of the sun, which is an exact precise time every year, and not by the moon which is of darkness and the timing hops around like an Easter bunny.

"Your glorying is not good. Don't you know that a little leaven leavens the whole loaf?" (1 Corinthians 5:6)

> Leaven makes bread rise and puff up. It's symbolic of evil. Satan was puffed up with pride, and it became his downfall and he became evil.

"Behold the Lamb of God which take away the sin of the world." (John 1:29)

"John looked on Jesus as he walked, and he said behold the Lamb of God." (John 1:36)

> Today Christ is our Passover, and He looks in our hearts to see if we accepted what He has done for us. He is the Lamb without blemish! Satan cannot touch Christ's people who are Christians covered by Christ's blood and sacrifice. But once people stop being a servant, and they walk out the door to work for Satan, the protection ceases to cover them.

"You cannot drink the cup of the Lord and the cup of devils: you cannot be partakers of the Lord's table, and the table of devils." (1 Corinthians 10:21)

"This is an ordinance to be observed forever." (Exodus 12:24)

It is the sacrifice of the Lord's Passover. And the destroyer was not allowed to go into the houses with the blood on the doorposts. At midnight, Pharaoh rose up and heard a great cry throughout all the land, from his throne to his servants, and to the captives who were in the dungeon. There was not a house without a covering of blood on the doorposts that did not have one dead. With this, Pharaoh told Moses to take the people and go. *(See Reference*: Exodus 12: 22- 39) The Red Sea stopped the Egyptians from taking the people of Israel back into Egypt, and drowned all them who served Pharaoh and his evil lust, that not one remained alive. *(See Reference:* Exodus 14: 25- 31)

"He cast upon them the fierceness of His anger, Wrath, and indignation, and trouble. By sending evil angels among them." (Psalms 78:49)

"And killed all the firstborn in Egypt." (Psalms 78:51)

"After the manner of Egypt." (Isaiah 10:26)

"The thing that has been, is the thing that shall be; and that which is done is that which shall be done: and there is no new thing under the sun." (Ecclesiastes 1:9)

Lights of Fire

> Supernatural slaughters happened thousands of years ago, and they happen today! But the evil angels were told not to touch His anointed. (*See reference:* Psalms 105: 15) Egypt was almost a total ruin when Israel departed. After all the signs that the Lord gave the Pharaoh, it's even a bigger phenomenon that he thought he could keep Israel from serving their Creator. It's written that there will be others that will try. It was poetic justice with the Pharaoh killing the Lord's firstborn sons, and the Lord repaying the favor to the Pharaoh's firstborn sons.

"For as the children are partakers of flesh and blood, He Himself is also likewise took part of the same; that through death He might destroy him that had the power of death, that is, the devil." (Hebrews 2: 14)

> He didn't ask us to do anything that He didn't do Himself and gave us the choice of who we are going to follow.

"For even Christ our Passover is sacrificed for us." (1 Corinthians 5:7)

"At midnight there was a great cry." (Exodus 12: 29-30)

DAVID'S NUMBERING

"And again the anger of the Lord was kindled against Israel, and He moved David against them to say, go number Israel and Judah." (2 Samuel 24:1)

> Being that there's nothing new under the sun, the mentality always is, "I got your number." When a ruler with a lot of power gathers information about the nation's population, it never goes well for the people. If anyone does something the ruler doesn't like, he will have their number to retaliate.

"And Satan stood up against Israel, and provoked David to number Israel." (1 Chronicles 21:1)

> More than likely the children of Israel were like the people today. Destroying and killing one another for money, the pleasures of intoxication, gang members using brutalities to control their territory, coveting other people's riches, and the thing that coveting always leads to; the intoxication of the power to rule the world. From one end of the Spectrum to the other end with bribes.

The devil took Jesus up to an exceeding high mountain, and showed him all the kingdoms of the world, and all the power of them; he said all these things will I give You if You will fall down and worship me. Then Jesus said unto him, "get behind Me Satan: for it is written, thou shalt worship the Lord thy God and Him only shall you serve." (*See references:* Matthew 4: 8-10 and Luke 4: 5-8)

> This shows the coveting of Satan for the world and the power of it.

David told Joab to go number the children of Israel. Joab told David that the Lord could increase the people a hundredfold if He wanted to. He asked David why he would want to do this thing against Israel. But Satan had a good hold on David, and he prevailed and Joab went to number Israel. After the numbering was done, David knew he had sinned in doing this. David asked the Lord to forgive him. And the Lord sent a message back to David with three options. 1. Three years of famine. 2. Three months of being destroyed by Israel's enemies. 3. Three days of fallen angels destroying Israel. David told the messenger that he wanted the Lord to choose because he knew that the Lord has great mercy. He said, but just don't let me fall into the hand of man. (*See references:* 1 Chronicles 21: 2-13 and 2nd Samuel 24: 2-14)

> What David was saying is that he didn't want man's decision to make the matter worse. He knew the Lord would choose the most just and merciful punishment.

The Lord chose to send a pestilence of the fallen angels. And when the angel stretched out his hand upon Jerusalem to destroy it, the Lord repented Him of the evil. The Lord told the angel it is enough, stay now your hand. And the angel stood by the threshing place. And David went to build an altar unto the Lord so that the plague would stop.

David could not go to Gibeon where Moses had an altar for the Lord, because he was scared out of his mind over this destroying angel. After David built an altar, he offered burnt offerings and peace offerings and called upon the Lord. And the Lord answered him with fire from heaven upon the altar, of the burnt offering. And the Lord commanded the destroying angel to put his sword back into his sheath. (*See references:* 1 Chronicles 21: 14-30 and 2 Samuel 24: 15-25)

> The Lord stopped the destroying angel before the three days were up. But David wanted to make sure he made the offering so the destroying angel wouldn't finish his job. After the Lord accepted the offering with fire from heaven, the plague stayed out from Israel. The angels were so brutal that it must've reached the Lord's heart, that he had to stop it before the three days were done. 70,000 Israelites were destroyed before it was over. (1 Chronicles 21:14) The Lord didn't do this to people who didn't deserve it. He has a way of reaching His people to make them reconsider their evil works, like with David. If someone wants to take part in destroying His people, He can let them fall into the hands of a mighty destroying angel. Three days of destroying angels also give us a view of how scary a supernatural attack and slaughter can be. It would appear that the devil is in charge of these angels when the slaughters take place.
>
> "The destroyer." (Exodus 12: 23)
>
> "Evil angels." (Psalm 78: 49)
>
> The larger slaughters have more angels? Dyatlov Pass Incident probably only needed one? Beware: don't take part in projects of destruction against our Creator's children.

"It's a fearful thing to fall into the hands of the living God." (Hebrews 10:31)

THE ANGELS OF SODOM AND GOMORRAH

Abraham sat at the door of the tent on a hot day when three men appeared unto him. He bowed himself to the ground and asked them to wait until he prepares bread and brings water to them. He dressed a calf, took butter and milk and set it before them, and they did eat. (*See reference:* Genesis 18: 1-8)

> Abraham knew this was the Lord and two angels.

"And the Lord said, shall I hide from Abraham that thing which I do? He told him that He heard the great cries from Sodom and Gomorrah, and their sin was very grievous." (Genesis 18: 17-21)

> The Lord, when He hears His children are being hurt because of wicked people, He becomes very angry. Without the people in Sodom following the Lord's Commandments, it was inevitable that a supernatural slaughter would be on the way.

Abraham had a nephew named Lot, which went to this area and built these cities. It was hard for Abraham to believe that the land that he gave to Lot would become so wicked that it would need to be destroyed. However, Abraham knew that the people who were mixing in with Lot were trouble makers, so he had moved them away from him before it ruined the morals of his own people. (*See reference:* Genesis 13: 7)

"Abraham was a very rich man." (Genesis 13: 2)

> Abraham was wise enough to segregate himself from the proselytizing accusations that are always made from those kinds of people. Those kinds of people will divide a nation and destroy it from within. When they mix in with Christians, the corruption spreads like leaven or a wild fire. Christians need our Creators laws to keep "Sodom and Gomorrah" from happening. "Sodom and Gomorrah" shows what happens when you remove Him and his Commandments from the public eye. Christians will break His laws quickly enough, without destroying, and removing His laws from the people. The law of covetousness is usually the first law broken.

"And Lot lifted up his eyes and beheld." (Genesis 13:10)

"Everyone from the least even unto the greatest is given to covet." (Jeremiah 8:10)

David was a man after the Lord's own heart, and David had Uriah killed because he lifted up his eyes and beheld Uriah's wife. (*See reference:* 2 Samuel 11:2; 15)

The two angels turned their faces toward Sodom. When they got to Sodom, somehow Lot also knew they were angels. He bowed himself to the ground and asked them to come to his house for the night. They said no, they will sleep in the street. But Lot got them to come to his house after pleading with them. Not long after, the men of the city show up and demanded to have these men. Lot offered his two daughters instead. But they said no, they want the two men. The two angels grabbed a hold of Lot and pulled him inside. The angels blinded the men of the city so that they struggled to find the door. The angels told Lot the cities were going to be destroyed because of all the cries that came before the Lord's Face. The next day, Lot tried to get his sons-in-law ready to get out of the city, but they refused to believe that there would be an actual judgment. For Abraham's sake, and the Lord being merciful, the angels set Lot's two daughters and his wife outside the city. After they set them down, Lot's wife looked back, and she turned into a pillar of salt. The angels left Lot to go into a small city. The Lord destroyed the city around him, and his daughters so that Lot feared to live there, and he went up into the mountains. (*See reference:* Genesis 19:1-30)

> A lot of supernatural things happen in these old writings. 1. Lot saw something to give him the idea that these were angels. 2. These angels were able to blind all those men. 3. They used some kind of force to push all of the men away from the door. 4. The angels pick up Lot's family and set them outside the city somehow. 5. The Lord rained down fire and brimstone. 6. Lot's wife became a pillar of salt. 7. The Lord brought the little city down around Lot's head.
>
> Like Abraham, Lot had to have seen something about these angels that the men of the city didn't. The angels were able to blind them and move them away from the door. Then they picked up Lot's family and set them outside the city. It would be logical to assume that Lot's wife started walking back to Sodom in her desire to return to what she enjoyed. When one starts walking back, then the others will follow. Once they saw she was in a stationary spot as a pillar of salt, there was nothing else to do but move on. The angels did not fight them about going into that little city, but the Lord drove them out with fear. Only for Abraham's sake did the Lord do this. But somehow, He was able to destroy that little city with Lot in it. It scared the wits out of Lot, so much so that he decided he didn't want to live there anymore. Sometimes the Lord gives His people enough rope so they can learn from their mistakes, and their cries of oppression must happen to bring their obedience back to doing what is right. Lot's sons-in-law took everything as a mockery, and the most puzzling phenomenon is how people can't see what's happening around them and is right in front of their eyes. This is a phenomenon of being even more blind than the soldiers that Elisha led to Samaria.

"Even if an angel from heaven preach any other gospel unto you than what the Holy Spirit gave, let him be accursed." (Galatians 1: 8)

> The verse in Galatians is added to bring home the warning of how you entertain strangers, and that it doesn't only apply for good angels which were treated shamefully in this chapter.

"Be careful how you entertain strangers, because some entertained angels unaware." (Hebrews 13:2)

THE FOUR HORNS OF SLAUGHTER

1.) I looked, and behold, One Who sat upon a white cloud, - - - - the Son of Man, having on His head a golden crown, and in His hand a sharp sickle. 2.) Another angel came out of the Temple, crying with a loud voice to Him that sat on the cloud, "Thrust in Thy sickle, and reap: for the time is come for Thee to reap; for the harvest of the earth is ripe." 3.) Another angel came out of the Temple which is in heaven, he also having a sharp sickle. 4.) Another angel came out from the altar, which had power over fire; and cried with a loud cry to him that had the sharp sickle, saying, "Thrust in your sharp sickle, and gather the clusters of the vine of the earth: for her grapes are fully ripe." And the angel thrust in the sickle into the earth, and gathered the vine of the earth, and cast it into the great winepress of the wrath of God. And out of the winepress came blood, even unto the horse's bridles. (*See reference:* Revelation 14:14-20)

> Why would there be so much wrath from our Creator, to provoke Him to bring blood up to the horse's bridle? For the same reason, He allowed the evil angel to have fun with the nine Russian hikers. They support a government that doesn't believe in our Creator or wants Him around. When leaders force Him away from His children, and His children choose those kinds of leaders, it makes Him angry. Our Creator steps back and lets evil move in. There are always leaders and fools who come along and pick up where the Pharaoh of Egypt left off. Since the beginning of time, the fight and struggle for freedom have always been bloody with a lot of death. This future bloody war with our Creator, described in the opening of this chapter is certainly no exception. The only exception of this last war is that it may be the bloodiest of all wars. Pushing our Creator out of the way and breaking His Commandments is always the start of evil things to come.

Lights of Fire

"After these things I saw four angels standing on the four corners of the earth, holding the four winds of the earth." (Revelation 7:1)

"The Four Horns." (Zachariah 1:18)

"The Four Angels." (Revelation 14:14-20)

"The Four Winds." (Revelation 7:1)

"The Four Horses." (Revelation 6:2-8)

> The number four pertains to Earth. East, West, North, and South. Winter, Summer, Spring and Fall. Morning, Evening, Noon, and Night. Creatures of the water, creatures of the air, creatures underground, and creatures above ground. The Four Horns of Slaughter will cover what brings this future bloody war to earth. Horned animals will use the power of their horns to move things. This chapter will cover the four horns that move people, but we will start with the modern-day fulfillments of prophecy leading up to the slaughters.

The Lord appeared unto Abram, and said, "your name shall not be called Abram any more, but your name shall be called Abraham; for a father of many nations have I made you." (See reference: Genesis 17:5- 6)

> Abraham's son was named Isaac. The Lord gave Isaac's wife Rebekah the prophecy of the nations and the superpowers in the last days. The two children that she would be giving birth to were two very different kinds of people.

Isaac's wife Rebecca had two children struggling within her womb, so she inquired of the Lord why this is happening. The Lord told her two nations are in her womb and two manner of people shall be separated from her bowels. One people shall be stronger than the other people, and the elder shall serve the younger. (*See reference:* Genesis 25:21-23)

> The Communist Manifesto refers to this as, the Proletariat, or the working class, serving the Bourgeoisie, or the Capitalist who pays the workers as little as they can get away with.
> Russia, the Proletariat elder, serving America the Bourgeoisie Capitalists. If Russia intends to change that, they will need disruptive instigators mixing in with America's capitalism workers.

Abram was very rich in cattle, in silver, and in gold. And there was strife between the herdsmen of Abrams cattle and the herdsmen of Lot's cattle. (And a [disruptive people] dwelled among them.) (*See reference:* Genesis 13: 2- 8)

> The two superpowers in the end days would be struggling together in the Cold War. The freedom-loving nation, against the people of an oppressed, controlled, socialist nation. The two manners of people are God-fearing people, as opposed to atheistic people. Esau which was the eldest will serve the younger which is Jacob. Common sense tells you the wealthier nation is going to get the poorer nation to do what they want because of the wealth. That's a fact of life, and it doesn't take too much of an imagination to know which nations that would be. There is a statement in the book titled, *The 5000 Year Leap*, by W. Cleon Skousen, principles of freedom 101: The Challenge: xvii- - - the United States represents approximately 5% of the world's population but has created more wealth than all the rest of the world combined.

"The wealthy nation that dwells without care, which have neither gates or bars, which dwells alone. - - - I will bring the four winds on the four quarters of heaven. - - - And in the last days, I will destroy the king and the princes, and bring the captivity again." (Jeremiah 49: 31 + 36 + 38-39)

> It also does not take too much imagination to know which nation dwells alone, surrounded by two large bodies of water, in a carefree world. "The four winds of heaven" which opened this chapter is an important time frame. The prophecy in Jeremiah sounds like the president of this nation is going to be destroyed, and the captivity is going to be brought upon the people. Without a free world, you have oppression. When you look from a satellite down on North and South Korea, you can see the light of freedom and the darkness of oppression between those two nations. Like its says in the *Ballard of the Green Berets*, "fighting for those who are oppressed." The wealthy nation that stood for freedom around the world, had the Creator of the heavens and the earth standing by her side. By this point, there should be an understanding of which two nations we are talking about. The nine very intelligent, strong-willed, nice, good-humored hikers stood with the wrong people. Supernatural slaughters happen in that nation because of its oppressive, atheistic, evil ways. Our Heavenly Father didn't think it was so nice of the hikers to help with a program to destroy His children who trusted and acknowledged Him. The supernatural slaughter in Egypt shows how He feels about those who touch His firstborn. More than likely there were a lot of nice Egyptians, like the daughter of the Pharaoh who was nice to Moses. The two manner of people: The children of Jacob living in the United States of America, with all the blessings of our Creator by a God-fearing people. And the children of Esau living Russia in darkness, with a social system ruled by tyrants, and having nothing to do with our Creator and His Laws. But it would seem that the U.S.A. is moving in that direction.

"Touch not My anointed." (Psalms 105:15)

> Before bringing in the Four Horns of Slaughter, one more event should help nail down this Cold War struggle between the United States, and Russia which is referred to in Genesis 25:21-23.

"These are the four spirits of the heavens which go forth from standing before the Lord of all the earth." (Zachariah 6:5)

"The black horses go into the north country." (Zachariah 6:6)

"Black like an oven because of the terrible famine." (Lamentation 5:10)

Jack Randle

"The white horses go forth after them." (Zachariah 6:6)

"His Name is called the Word of God, and the armies which are in heaven followed Him upon white horses." (Revelation 19:13-14)

"These that go toward the north Country have quieted My Spirit in the north Country." (Zachariah 6:8)

> President Reagan made the declaration to President Gorbachev that the United States will outspend the Soviet Union in the Cold War. The Star Wars program was one such declaration the Soviet Union couldn't financially out counter in this strategic power struggle. This brought about the black horses of famine that went into the north country of Russia. With the black horse of famine bringing about the collapse of the Soviet Union in 1991, it brought the white horses of the Word of God into Russia. The Word of God was not allowed into the Soviet Union before 1991. And that's what quieted our Creators Spirit in the North country. (*See reference:* Zachariah 6: 8)

"And His Name is called the Word of God." (Revelation 19:13)

> Fools can take His Name in vain like the Pharaoh, but those fools will end up in worse shape than the nine Russian hikers, after the manner of Egypt.

Then I lifted up my eyes, and saw, and behold four horns. These horns are come to (fray) terrify them. (*See references:* Zechariah 1: 18 + 21) Fray— Strong's Concordance Hebrew dictionary number 2729 (See Figure 7 below).

2729. חָרַד **chârad**, *khaw-rad'*; a prim. root; to *shudder* with terror; hence to *fear*; also to *hasten* (with anxiety):—be (make) afraid, be careful, discomfit, fray (away), quake, tremble.

Figure 7. Meaning of the word "fray"

> The word "terrify" fits better than Fray, and documents where the word comes from. More fitting when you're talking about the four horns of slaughter. The hiker that was laying in the creek without internal injuries or hypothermia would be a sign of that terror. The four horns or powers that will move people: 1. Religion, 2. Political, 3. Educational, 4. Economy.

1. RELIGION HORN THAT MOVE PEOPLE

"The time is come that judgement must begin at the house of God: and if it begins first at us, what shall be the end of them that obey not the gospel of God?" (1 Peter 4:17)

> So the first horn that will be discussed, is where judgment will start: Religion. The Twin Towers in New York were taken down because of religion. Before hitting the Twin Towers, the quote: "Allahu Akbar" or "God is Greater" was shouted. Religion was able to move them to take the Twin Towers down, which was terrifying at the time.

"With men of other tongues and other lips will I speak unto this people; and yet for all that will they not hear Me saith the Lord." (1 Corinthians 14:21)

> That was a sign which has the same phenomenon around the event of the Russian hikers. The Lord was speaking to us in another tongue. And yet for all that people will not hear.

…hear the Word at My mouth, and give them a warning from Me… if the righteous man commits iniquity because you did not give him warning, the righteousness that he did will not be remembered; but his blood will I require at your hand. (*See reference:* Ezekiel 3: 17- 21)

> Here's the warning from His Word at His mouth.

"Woe be unto the pastors that destroy and scatter the sheep of my pasture! saith the Lord." (Jeremiah 23:1)

"Because with your lies you have made the heart of the righteous sad, whom I have not made sad, and strengthened the hands of the wicked, that he should not return from his wicked way, by promising him life:" (Ezekiel 13: 22)

> It was pointed out that Moses killed the Egyptian, and that he did not murder the Egyptian. To better illustrate, these underlined words are two very different Hebrew Words in the Strong's Concordance Dictionary. (See Figures 8, 9 and 10 below) Today, we have some pastors promising life to people that support evil and oppressive governments by saying that going to war breaks God's Commandment, "Thou shall not kill."

KILL

lest any finding him should *k* him	Gen 4:15	5221
and they will *k* me, but they will	Gen 12:12	2026
the place should *k* me for Rebekah	Gen 26:7	2026
himself, purposing to *k* thee	Gen 27:42	2026
and said, Let us not *k* him	Gen 37:21	5221
it be a son, then ye shall *k* him	Ex 1:16	4191
intendest thou to *k* me, as thou	Ex 2:14	2026
LORD met him, and sought to *k* him	Ex 4:24	4191
Israel shall *k* it in the evening	Ex 12:6	7819
your families, and *k* the passover	Ex 12:21	7819
to *k* this whole assembly with	Ex 16:3	4191
us up out of Egypt, to *k* us	Ex 17:3	4191
Thou shalt not *k*	Ex 20:13	7523
or a sheep, and *k* it, or sell it	Ex 22:1	2873
I will *k* you with the sword	Ex 22:24	2026
thou shalt *k* the bullock before	Ex 29:11	7819

Figure 8: The word "kill" in Strong Concordance #s 7523 and 2026

7523. רָצַח **râtsach,** *raw-tsakh'*; a prim. root; prop. to *dash in pieces*, i.e. *kill* (a human being), espec. to *murder*:—put to death, kill, (man-) slay (-er), murder (-er).

Figure 9: Strong's Concordance # 7523 Hebrew word for murder

Lights of Fire

2026. הָרַג **hârag**, *haw-rag'*; a prim. root; to *smite* with deadly intent:—destroy, out of hand, kill, murder (-er), put to [death], make [slaughter], slay (-er), × surely.

Figure 10: Strong's Concordance # 2026 Hebrew word for kill

> And at the same time, they condemn the righteous man for killing the man that supports evil. Killing men in war is not murder. Our Creator did not change His Word after Emmanuel came to earth, and took part in flesh and blood the same as us.

"For as much as the children are partakers of flesh and blood, He also Himself likewise took part of the same;" (Hebrews 2:14).

"Jesus Christ the same yesterday, and today, and forever." (Hebrews 13:8)

"For I am the Lord, I change not." (Malachi at 3:6)

"Your father Abraham rejoice to see My day: and he saw it, and was glad." (John 8:56)

"For God is not the author of confusion." (1 Corinthians 14: 33)

> He is not the author of confusion. He is not going to change His Word all around on us. That confusion comes from pastors that are ignorant of His Word. The blood ordinances and the shadows of those things that He became are done away with. (*See reference:* Colossians 2: 14- 17) That has nothing to do with promising life to a person that supports evil. What did our Creator say about war and the killing of soldiers, or the Egyptian who Moses killed?

Sheba called for a revolt against David, so Joab and Abishai pursued after him. When they came to the city where he took refuge, Joab started battering the wall to throw it down. Then a wise woman cried out and ask them if they never heard of the Word of God. Joab asked her to speak on, so she quoted our Creators Word. She told Joab, "When you come to a city to fight against it, proclaim peace first. Ask them what you're coming for, and if they will not give you what you ask, then go to war. The Lord will give it to you and you shall kill all the males in the city." (*See reference:* Deuteronomy 20: 10- 13)

> Probably the Lord's reasoning for killing all the males was so that they don't come and make battle again. Stand with evil and they will die with evil. The Egyptians took part in evil against our Creators people. Again, stand with evil and they will die with evil. They shall not be promised life when doing this.

"When the wise woman found out what Joab wanted, she went and cut Sheba's head off and threw it over the wall to him." (2 Samuel 20:1-22)

> Stand with evil and we shall die with evil. The same yesterday, today, and forever. Hopefully, that helps to clear the understanding of the difference between murder and killing. The warning from Him has now been given. (*See reference:* Ezekiel 3: 17)

"Is not My Word like as a fire?" (Jeremiah 23:29)

"For our God is a consuming fire." (Hebrews 12:29)

"Aaron's two sons offered strange fire, and there went out fire from the Lord and devoured them, and they died before the Lord." (Leviticus 10: 1-2)

> That is a dire warning for those of us that handle His Word. Our Creator doesn't want us destroying or scattering the sheep of His pasture.

"I am against those that hunt the souls to make them fly." (Ezekiel 13:20)

"Stand in the battle in the day of the Lord." (Ezekiel 13: 5)

"Put on the whole armor of God, that you may be able to stand in the evil day, and having done all, to stand." (Ephesians 6: 13)

"And the devil went to make war with those which keep the Commandments of God, and have the Testimony of Jesus Christ." (Revelation 12: 17)

> We have a war coming that we are going to need some armor for! And if we don't have the Commandments of God or the Testimony of Jesus Christ, there sure is no reason to be teaching His Word! There's a lot more that could be said on that terrifying horn, but we will move on to the next horn of slaughter.

2. POLITICAL HORN THAT MOVE PEOPLE

"These are the things that you shall do; speak you every man the truth to his neighbor; execute the judgment of truth and peace in your gates: And let none of you imagine evil in your hearts against his neighbor; And love no false oath: for all these are things that I hate, saith the Lord." (Zachariah 8: 16- 17)

> Don't make lies to deceive people. Execute the judgment of righteousness to all people, don't imagine evil like Jezebel with her covetous murder, and don't declare a lie as the truth in our Creator's Name, like the two witnesses of Jezebel. This horn comes to power with covetousness, which, leads to murder, and leads to a supernatural slaughter in the end.

"Mary poured very expensive ointments on Jesus' feet, and Judas Iscariot asked why the ointment was not sold for money and given to the poor. He said this not because he cared for the poor, but because he was a thief and he had the bag which bears the money." (John 12: 3-6)

> It was said that the United States held its freedom longer than any other civilization. But as soon as the people discover how they can get free things from those in power, they sell their freedom for whatever they are offering. They will buy votes with healthcare, free housing, free food, and anything else that they can buy vote with. This money does not belong to them, but they know where they can get it. They covet the riches of the profitable citizens and tell the people how the rich must pay their fair share. But when coveting starts, there will never be enough riches for them to take. But just like Judas Iscariot, who betrayed Jesus to death for money, the same danger of voting for a covetous person into office is just as dangerous. Nothing new under the sun. They are always talking about taking from the rich, and giving to the poor as Judas did.

"Ahab was a king over Israel and he coveted the vineyard of Naboth. Ahab tried to buy the vineyard from Naboth, but Naboth told Ahab that the Lord forbids selling the inheritance of his father's unto him." (1 Kings 21: 1-2)

> The vineyard would be his children's birthright, inheritance, and heritage. But Ahab coveted this vineyard, and the breaking of one Commandment led to breaking more Commandments.

Lest there be any fornicator, or profane person, as Esau, who for one morsel of meat sold his birthright. (Hebrews 12:16)

Esau sold his birthright unto Jacob. (Genesis 25: 33)

> The Constitution of the United States is our birthright, and heritage from our Creator. Esau sold the birthright to Jacob, which gave America its wealth and blessings. The prophecy of the elder, Esau, Russia, to serve the younger, Jacob, the U.S.A. our heritage and birthright from our Creator.

Jezebel Ahab's wife saw that Ahab was very sad, and asked him what is wrong. He told her that he wanted Naboth's vineyard, but Naboth wouldn't sell it to him. Jezebel said, "do you not govern the kingdom?" Arise, and eat, and let your heart be merry: I will get it for you. Then Jezebel contacted two corrupt men and told them to witness against Naboth, saying that he blasphemed God and the king. They brought Naboth before the people in the court, and these two corrupt men witnessed against him. So the people took Naboth out and stoned him that he died. Then Ahab went down to take possession of Naboth's vineyard. (*See reference:* 1 Kings 21:1-16)

> When someone testifies falsely against someone else in a court of law, if it's found out, the same judgment of the accused is to be pronounced on that person that testified falsely. (*See reference:* Deuteronomy 19: 18- 21) When a ruler is saying that they got to take from the rich, you know Jezebel's way of thinking is not far behind. What Jezebel did is classified as murder. While on the subject of murder. John Adams, one of this nation's founding fathers once said, "an immoral people cannot inherit the Constitution."

The second amendment was passed so that the citizens could protect themselves, and the lives of their loved ones. It was not to be abridged. With all the immoral people going on shooting sprees, it brings home the message of what John Adams was saying. And while we are on the subject of short-circuiting the Constitution, we must discuss the foresight of it.

A crisis came up in a country, and the great leader told its citizens that the Constitution could not have foreseen the crisis. The Constitution was suspended, and martial law was introduced. Today you hear people in the United States saying that the Constitution could not have foreseen the technology of today. The people saying this have no intelligence on the subject, or they are very evil people. The Reichstag German parliament building burned, and Hitler used the event to convince President Hindenburg to declare a state of emergency, suspending important Constitutional safeguards. The decree was a key step in the establishment of the Nazi dictatorship. Germany became a police state in which citizens enjoyed no guaranteed basic rights, and the SS, the elite guard of the Nazi state, wielded increasing more authority through its control over the police. Ron Paul, whatever you think about him, makes a very good statement. "We are too easy to give up our rights." The Constitution was designed against evil people like Ahab and Jezebel. The Constitution never changes its safeguards against evil dictatorships or the rule of law against evil people. Evil people use technology, and the excuse of technology to destroy the safeguards of the Constitution, along with the rules of law. But the Constitution is firm with the rules of law against the evils of men. If there is anything that the Constitution could not have foreseen, it is how evil and stupid the people are today. What else can be said about that kind of dangerous talk, and those that believe it? One more statement to make in this political horn. The Electoral vote was to keep things fair among the American citizens to some extent. Giving people in the country the same say over who is President as the people in the city. When a politician says that we should go by the popular vote, they are labeling themselves. They are saying that they believe in mob rule, and the mobs should dictate who goes into office. We were never intended to have a dangerous government of mob rule. Now we move to the next terrifying horn.

3. EDUCATIONAL HORN THAT MOVE PEOPLE

The invisible things of Him from the creation of the world are seen by the things that are already made, - - -They became vain in their imaginations, and their foolish heart was darkened. Professing themselves to be wise, they became fools and changed the glory of the incorruptible God into an image made like to corruptible man, and to birds, and four-footed beasts, and creeping things. Who changed the truth of God into a lie, and worshipped and served the creature more than the Creator? (*See reference:* Romans 1: 20- 25)

> How many schools are learning about global warming, which is now being called climate change? They're taking all the things that our Creator has made, and with all their instruments, they profess themselves to be wise, taking their man-made images in science to teach others a "science" based on lies. Man is causing climate change to the earth and something needs to be done. The fact is that every time a baby is born, the baby contributes to the climate change crisis. The more babies the more factories for the materials associated with the baby, along with energy and fuel that it takes. Solar, wind, and algae will not solve the problem, and they're not meant to. For a long time, China had regulations on how many children their people could have. A two-child limit was dictated to the people. Germany's idea in the 1930s was to get rid of people that were putting a drag on their society. 1. When elderly people lived their lives, it's time to go. The health-care system couldn't afford to try to keep them healthy. 2. The dangerous citizens needed to be eliminated. Those that would not go along with the final solution. 3. Citizens that were not helping the cause were a waste of space. They needed people who were going to make Germany a great 1,000 year Reich. One dictator in China had the idea to starve people to death, which was the most effective way to eliminate approximately a million people.

A new Pharaoh arose which knew not Joseph. And he said, "behold the people of Israel are greater and mightier than the Egyptians. Let us the deal wisely with them; lest they multiply, and we lose control of them. So they put task masters over them and made them serve with rigor. Then they started murdering our Creators firstborn. (*See reference:* Exodus 1: 8- 22)

Lights of Fire

There's nothing new under the sun. (*See reference:* Ecclesiastes 1:9)

> History has always shown how oppressive rulers operate to control the population. Are teachers teaching the final solution? Man worries more about the creation than the Creator. Our Creator has His hand on the thermostat of the world. Like maybe the O-Zone hole opens and closes to let the heat in and out. The oceans heat and cools, to control the weather. The cycles of the sun control the weather. Our Creator has the capability to get our attention, and that too is an inconvenient truth. The media has a big part in educating and moving the people. They have a lot of influence on the way people think and believe. There is no investigative reporting anymore. The media has the platform to bring forth the global agenda. People in our government through a program called, "Fast and furious" supplied automatic weapons to the drug cartel in Mexico. Brian Terry an American citizen was murdered by these automatic weapons. His family was never able to find out why a government program would do this. The media reported that the program was started by the previous administration, effectively covering up, smearing, and dividing Americans to make the slaughter story go away. "It wasn't our team that started the program." They use statements like that to cover, smear, and divide! Abraham Lincoln quoted the Bible when he said, "a nation divided cannot stand."

"Every kingdom divided against itself is brought to desolation." (Matthew 12:25)

> Poor against rich, citizens against police officers, black against white, and a political party against a political party. The propaganda machines have done a fantastic job of dividing American citizens. We do have some good investigative reporting, but the propaganda machines drown them out.
>
> After the Libyan war when Muammar Gaddafi was overthrown, a lot of American weapons were still in the country. Most of the countries pulled all their personnel out of Libya because it was very dangerous. One report said Ambassador Stevens was there at a very dangerous time to stop those weapons from getting into the wrong hands. Another report said these weapons were going into Syria. At the time, the push was to remove Bash al-Assad of Syria from the presidency.

They were pushing to arm the rebels in Syria, but most of these weapons were going into the same hands of those who slaughtered Ambassador Stevens. During this slaughter they had unarmed drones flying overhead watching this battle rage on without helping. The obvious conclusion is that Ambassador Stevens wasn't thinking like the dictators, and he paid the ultimate price. We had two Navy SEALs that disobey orders to stand down, and they went to help Ambassador Stevens. After one unarmed drone ran out of fuel, they sent out the next unarmed drone to watch this battle. The battle went on over 13 hours and it cost two Navy SEALs their life. They could've been our brother, father, or son, the same as Brian Terry, the border guard. The propaganda machines pushed the lie of a video causing a spontaneous riot that murdered the four American citizens.

They pushed the lie of a video being the cause, and they never investigated the real atrocity of those murders. Why? Again those American citizens could've been your father, brother, or son. How can Americans claim to be patriotic, and not care about finding out how these things happen? Using the excuse of national security is the best way of not losing support for a global agenda. If German citizens would've found out about the atrocities in Nazi Germany, no doubt much needed support would've been lost to the cause. The people looking over the national security, and leaking national security information, were to be taken out and shot, after a court of law convicts them, for obvious reasons. Measures were always taken to prevent evil people from getting away with murder, and putting our nation at risk at the same time. The first amendment of the Constitution protects offensive speech, which is very important and why it made the list on the Bill of Rights as number one. It gives people the right to express their views without retribution. Assuming that was the reason for pushing the video propaganda. Benjamin Franklin made the statement when asked, "what kind of government did you give us." He answered, "a republic if you can keep it." We have a lot of enemies that want to destroy our government from within!

"In the latter times some shall depart from the faith, giving heed to seducing spirits and doctrines of devils; speaking lies in hypocrisy; having their conscience seared with a hot iron." (1 Timothy 4:1-3)

> Our Creator controls the weather, and He sees the evil doctrines, with their conscience being seared about their fellow citizens being murdered. That touched on the terror of the educational horn.

4. ECONOMY, THE LAST HORN

"And where the Spirit of the Lord is, there is liberty." (2 Corinthians 3:17)

> In the *Declaration of Independence*, it is written: We hold these Truths to be self-evident, that all men are created equal, that they are endowed by their Creator with certain unalienable Rights, that among these are Life, Liberty, and the Pursuit of Happiness — We are endowed by our Creator with certain unalienable rights. Our independence from England and the tyrannical king gave us our Constitution. The goal was to give us freedoms from being controlled by our government. To give us life, liberty, and the pursuit of happiness. Those rights come from our Creator.

"If any man will not work, neither should he eat." (2 Thessalonians 3:10)

> That is a certain unalienable right that comes from our Creator. Our Creator gave everyone the right to starve to death if they don't want to work. A moral person will take care of the elderly and the handicapped. That is talking about people capable of working.

"If any provide not for his own, and especially for those of his own house, he has denied the faith, and is worse than infidel." (1 Timothy 5:8)

> The "state" level is fine for taking care of one's own house. But not for the Judas Iscariots at the federal level. Also, there are lots of nice organizations to make donations that help to take care of the less fortunate, which people of morals will support. Welfare and the war against poverty at the federal level, was started in the 1960s and will run us all into poverty There are too many Judas Iscariots. Healthcare is not a right from our Creator. So healthcare from our Federal government is not a Constitutional right. If we choose not to take care of our health, that's up to us. But with the government paying for our health, they will need to put controls and rules on our lives.

> They cannot give us the liberty to keep our bad habits and run up the costs for healthcare on everybody. Again the states have the right to provide healthcare, like the Massachusetts bankrupt healthcare catastrophe. But the federal government didn't have the right to bail them out. If you don't allow them to learn from their mistakes, they will keep making them. They have a God-given right to fail and learn from that failure. What happened with Massachusetts' healthcare system will happen with the whole country! It's easier to leave a state than to leave a country because of bad policies. The control is closer to "We The People," at the state level. The National Healthcare System is about 25% of the economy and will bankrupt us, along with giving us our biggest loss of liberty in our nation's history. Our Creator wanted us to have the liberty to learn from our mistakes, and not be controlled by tyrants!

"Know the truth, and the truth shall make you free." (John 8:32)

"Where the Spirit of the Lord is, you have the spirit of liberty." (2 Corinthians 3:17)

"Stand fast therefore in the liberty whereas Christ has made us free." (Galatians 5:1)

> The national debt clock is over $20 trillion, and in 2008 it was 10 trillion. $1 trillion is a lot of money, and if the interest rate goes up there's no way we will stand good for that money. Our government relies on revenue from our workforce, which they call GDP. Pensions are being hurt by the low interest rates, but at the same time if the interest rates are raised, the interest on the national debt will be too high to make good on it. With higher interest rates, even in the most robust economy we will not be able to pay the interest on that debt. Anyone that knows the numbers, knows this, and numbers do not lie. It works the same as a credit card, only it's our national credit at risk. We have people in the global community that want this country to go bankrupt for one important agenda.

"Cast in your lot among us; let us all have one purse." (Proverbs 1:14)

> A one world currency…

The seven heads are seven mountains. Ten horns are ten Kings. These have one mind. (*See reference:* Revelation 17: 9- 13)

> "Seven mountains" – seven continents; "One mind" – world agreements.

> The economy will take us into a one world government. If our dollar does not fail, nobody will want to have one purse with one currency. The horns will push this agenda, with Americans finding out how it feels to live in a third world country. All because we are selling our birthright for a bowl mush. The next fight for freedom will be real bloody.

"The angel thrust in his sickle into the earth, and gathered the vine of the earth, and cast it into the great winepress of the wrath of God. And the winepress was trodden without the city, and blood came out of the winepress, even to the horse's bridals, by the space of a thousand and six hundred furlongs." (Revelation 14: 19-20)

Fret not yourself because of the evildoers, those wicked who plot against the just man, the Creator shall laugh at him: For He sees that his day is coming. *(See references:* Psalms 37: 1 + 12 + 13)

And what I say unto you I say unto all, "Watch." *(See reference:* Mark 13: 37)

"Blessed be the Lord my strength which teach my hands to war, and my fingers to fight:" (Psalms 144:1)

"Greater love hath no man than this, that a man lay down his life for his friends." (John 15:13)

This thank you goes to all the families who paid a price to keep this nation free! Thank you to the heroes of freedom, and may our Heavenly Father bless you!

SUMMARIZING THE MYSTERY AND THE EVIL BEHIND IT

Oppression has happened to civilizations from the beginning of time. People of the world looked at the United States as a beacon of hope for freedom. And Thomas Jefferson made a very interesting quote about freedom.

"God who gave us life, gave us liberty. Can the liberties of a nation be thought secure when we have removed their only firm basis, a conviction in the minds of the people, that these liberties are the gift of God? That they are not to be violated, but with His wrath?

Indeed, I tremble for my country when I reflect that God is just, that His justice cannot sleep forever. Thomas Jefferson 1781

It would appear that just like Egypt, the Soviet Union with its iron fist of oppression, saw first-hand God's Wrath.

He cast upon them the fierceness of His anger; Wrath, and indignation, and trouble, by sending evil angels among them. (Psalms 78: 49)

What the 1959, Russian investigators described as, "An Unknown Compelling Force."

The Unknown Compelling Force, which give some of the following questions.

> Question: What would force nine hikers to cut the tent and leave without their ski boots and coats?

Theory: Heat affects everybody in much the same way. When things are getting hot, most people will do their best to escape it. Especially if it's sudden extreme heat. References have been given in prior chapters as to the different kinds of fires and their effects. Most people will experience blindness to different degrees when looking into a welder's arc, but blindness would explain why they were walking instead of running. This would also explain why it looked like they were holding hands and combing the slope as though looking for something small. After being struck with blindness, the first instinct is not to start running when you can't see where you're going.

> Question: It was not normal for footprints to last almost a month in that kind of environment. How did it happen?

Theory: The supernatural heat from their bodies reacting or melting the snow, and then this reaction or refreeze into ice-packed snow help preserve the footprints.

> Question: How did Rustem Slobodin sustain head injuries on both sides of his head without puncture marks or scrapes on his arms and hands from the fall? Remember, the force was equivalent to a sixty-meter-per-hour accident.

Theory: A supernatural angel with a supernatural grip. This would not leave broken limbs, punctures, or scrape marks like falling and hitting a rock. The injury being on both sides of his head would be more like the grip of a supernatural angel's hand crushing his skull rather than the impact of one object. The theory of ice under his body, over five centimeters, is also explained as with the footprints. How much heat can a body give off naturally in those conditions?

Question: Why didn't Igor tell them to stay together as he did with the wild horses?

Theory: This angel used one hiker as bait which separated the group. Testing their survival skills, knowing they will not win, and having the pleasure of watching the struggle. It is documented that these angels are brutal and that they have great powers and might. The theory also explains how they came to die where they did that night, and how Igor was turned over after rigor mortis. Whatever Igor did that night was not against common sense. He was just up against the supernatural powers of a brutal angel.

Question: For what possible reason would a man climb up into a cedar tree then end up falling and breaking branches on the way down?

Theory: The common sense answer is that he climbed up there to look for something. The theory of him being a lookout for Rustem is as good a reason as any.

Question: What would make two hikers fall over a fire, at the same time, putting it out?

Theory: They were trying to conceal their position. It would be more likely than the theory that two of them, at the same time, getting the same biological symptom, that being the symptom that possesses people to fall into the fire when their half froze. The theory presented here has them being held down against their will when the angel reaches them. The reason for the severe burns.

Question: Why, after going to all the work of building the floor and getting clothes to set on, would they start taking a hike that they couldn't do in the daytime according to their diary?

Theory: They did not get six meters away from the floor voluntarily. There would be no logical reason for them to leave the floor like that.

Question: Why didn't the two hikers under the cedar tree go into the ravine, instead of staying there and freezing to death?

Theory: Both hikers had the duty of being a lookout, and to keep the fire going much like a lighthouse watchman. The light from the fire was for the hope of Zina seeing it, along with Igor and Rustem having a reference point to know where to come back. The light from the fire also helped the hikers to cut the trees for the floor. Both lookout hikers were in reasonably good shape until the fire was extinguished, so there was no reason to be relieved by anyone in the ravine.

Question: How did three of the four hikers get their bone-crushing injuries, equivalent to a sixty meter per hour accident, with no fractured limbs or puncture marks where their bones were broken?

Theory: They were crushed with the supernatural force of an angel. This would explain why they didn't fracture an arm or leg in a fall of that magnitude. With Lyuda's injury, they said she didn't last more than ten minutes after the injury happened. It's doubtful that these hikers were doing much walking around after receiving these bone-crushing injuries. Lyuda Dubinina, Kolya Thibault, Semyon Zolotaryov, and the man on the slope, Rustem Slobodin, none of them had any fractured limbs from a high impact fall.

> Question: How did Lyuda lose her tongue, lower teeth, and upper lip? And why were she and Semyon Zolotaryov missing their eyeballs?

Theory: This angel was mimicking a scorpion in defiance of any power over the fallen angels. The theory suggests the missing eyeballs were symbolic of them being blind, never to see again, and having their eternal life sucked out.

"King Zedekiah had his eyes put out." (2 Kings 25:6-7)

"Samson had his eyes put out." (Judges 16:21)

"As the torment of a scorpion." (Revelation 9:5)

Indians ran an awl into General Custer's ears as a gesture for him to hear in his next life. The evil angel may have done this for the intimidation to the people in this life which know the promises of God for eternity. I beheld Satan as lightning fall from heaven. Behold, I give you the power to tread on serpents and scorpions, and over all the power of the enemy. (*See reference:* Luke 10: 19)

"That seeing they may see, and not perceive; - - - lest at any time they should be converted, and their sins should be forgiven them." (Mark 4: 12)

"And anoint your eyes with eye-salve, that you may see." (Revelation 3: 18)

> **Question: How did Alexander Kolevatov end up to be with the other three hikers in the creek without any internal injuries or hypothermia?**

Theory: The cause of death was acute heart failure or heart attack. Something brought this on. Never having seen an attack of a brutal angel before, the 24-year-old hiker suffered a massive heart attack. This would explain how he ended up lying next to the other three hikers without having any internal injuries or hypothermia. How else could it be explained?

"It is documented that there will be a time when men's hearts will fail them for fear, and for looking after those things which are coming on the earth:" (Luke 21:26)

The sight of Lyuda made her father pass out when he came to see her body.

> **Question: It's obvious that people saw lights in the sky at the time of the Dyatlov Pass Incident! What is the connection, and why does it matter?**

Theory: The slaughter of Oreb, after the manner of Egypt. Gideon with his lamps, fire balls, orbs of lights at the mountain tops, or whatever you want to call them, were in connection with the slaughter of Egypt. It's documented that the slaughter was by evil angels. (Psalms 78:49) The signs around the nine Russian hikers look a lot like the method of operation of a brute beast or angel. These lights in the sky wouldn't go overlooked in connection with this mystery with the passing of time.

"Though hand joined in hand, the wicked shall not be unpunished: but the seed of the righteous shall be delivered." (Proverbs 11:21)

These hikers were friendly, had a sense of humor, and they were probably fun people to be around. They had one very big problem. The nuclear program they were participating in was for evil, oppressive, and tyrannical government against our Creator's children. Our Creator unleashes evil right back on the heads of those that participate, which is a very terrifying position to be in. Imagine going from the extreme heat to the extreme cold. Anyone who ever walked barefoot in snow knows how your feet become excruciatingly painful until you can't feel them anymore. This can happen while wearing boots. They struggle to do everything they can to stay alive, with the hope they can gather everybody together into the ravine. As they're trying to achieve this, the cold wind cuts right through their clothes. They struggle to do the simple things, as the cold penetrates right to the bone. As the night goes on they know their friends are dying one by one, and there's nothing they can do about it. They wonder how it is that these things are befalling them, and how nice it will be to be back home. When they get the warning that some evil beast is heading in their direction, they are puzzled about what is going on. They heard the scary stories of the region, and seeing the light from the fire disappear shortly after the warning, they become terrified. The night is anything but normal, and now their two friends are in subzero temperatures, in stronger wind, are now in total darkness under the cedar tree. This had to be serious knowing they won't survive long without having their coats and boots. As they sit in total darkness huddled together, they whisper among themselves, about what's going on and what they should do. After waiting for their friends to quietly show up, they know by this time something must have happened. Rustem took the flashlight with him, so they have no source of light, and the reason among themselves that there's nothing they can do for them. It would be like running into a room with deadly gas, only to end up like the people you're trying to help. It's an agonizing wait, but they still hope to see them coming with a flashlight. Meanwhile, the night visitor waits for the two to move up off the fire, and then it thrusts them back down on it again. Now they are being burned while freezing to death, but they struggle to get up. The pressure that holds them down is almost to the point where they can't breathe. If they intend to survive they must fight to get up, but in exhaustion they look at each other with the helpless look of defeat, knowing the outcome of death is inevitable. Both hikers fall into an exhausted sleep. The night visitor was not able to bait any of the other hikers to come help. After waiting for what seems to be hours for their two friends to show up, the suspenseful anticipation becomes too much, and Kolevatov decides to make the walk in the dark to the cedar, knowing he is the best dressed for it, but fearing for what he will find. Then finding both of his friends laying over the glowing embers, is heart-breaking, and terrifying at the same time. Looking around he thinks the night visitor left, but he still has a sense of danger. As he gathers the clothes, matches, with some other necessities, he wonders what kind of beast would do something like this? Taking these clothes from his friends is heart-wrenching, but he tries to respect them the best he can. These are friends that he was joking with, and having laughs with just hours before. Now the last four must share their friend's clothes trying not to come to the same fate. It will be 3:00 AM before too long, and the night visitor watches, thinking he will move in at the right time to finish the intoxicating sensation of the night. The best is yet to come and he savors the moment he moves in to end any chance of them having Salvation. The mouthwatering seduction of sucking their souls right out of their flesh bodies is more intoxicating than anything on this side hell. All the Pharaohs in Egypt, Jezebels in Israel, Hitler's in Germany, or the Globalists of the world, could match the intoxication of having these souls under their possession in that dimension. Waiting and watching for the right opportunity to end Salvation in the flesh. Semyon decides to write a record of the unimaginable night, and how their friends were attacked by something unexplainable. As one hiker holds a lit match so Semyon can see to write, this horrifying creature lights the whole ravine.

They're all frozen with fear waiting to see what this creature is going to do. It grabs Lyuda, and her blood-curdling scream turns into a gurgle as this creature crushes her chest. Beyond their wildest imagination, they see this creature spewing a foul-smelling fluid into her mouth, which is enough to paralyze the three of them with fear. Watching it suck her tongue out with the fluid, and the laser-like light from its eyes burns her eyes into puffs of vapor. Tossing her almost lifeless body like a rag doll, it moves to Kolevatov, and not taking much more than a touch from this hideous creature is enough to give him a heart attack. As he tosses his lifeless body, the other two watch in a paralyzed terror, waiting their turn to have the life squeezed out of them. As Semyon is being crushed, he squeezes tight on the pencil and diary. Their time to accept Christ as their Savior is now over. Those nine lost souls were worth more than all the gold in the world for Satan, and that angel. It would be an assumption that these evil angels probably compete against each other for lost souls, but why would it be any different for the evil in that dimension? The better an angel can scare people away from salvation, the mimicking, mocking, and brutality, the more prestige they may earn with Satan. The higher the status of an angel, the more they covet. The lust for this higher status and power being so seductive, it makes this mouthwatering game much more enticing. All for the love of coveting power and status.

"And the devil said unto Jesus, all this power will I give you, and the glory of them: for it is delivered unto me; and to whomsoever, I will I give it. If you, therefore, will worship me, all Shall be yours." (Luke 4: 6-7)

The devil is a liar to start with, but you can see the intoxicating lust involved in having power. To give to whom he wishes as long as they worship him, giving him the ultimate authority for power.

"And there was war in heaven: Michael and his angels fought against Satan; Satan fought with his angels against Michael, but Satan did not prevail. He was cast out into the earth, and his angels were cast out with him." (Revelations 12: 7- 9)

Trying to understand why people do evil things in this dimension, is just as hard as trying to understand why they do it in that dimension. The enticing phenomenon has coveting at the heart of it. Like the Pharaoh of Egypt fighting our Creator for the people of Israel. It's a battle that can't be won, but he had to try until Egypt was a total ruin. And even then the Pharaoh had to go after our Creator's people to get them back, and in the process losing more of his people in the Red Sea.

How do you explain a phenomenon like that? Or people like Jezebel, thinking they can just kill people to take whatever they want? Or the people of today lusting after the agendas, participating in the evil and having their conscience seared, not caring about the murders of fellow citizens? The same very sick thinking which has been described.

"Taking His Name in vain is done by disregarding His Commandments and the warnings that He put in His Word. And His Name is called the Word of God." (Revelation 19:13)

Taking His Word in vain is like attributing natural disasters to the nine hikers after knowing the facts of the case. There are repercussions for taking His Word in vain and not taking heed to His warnings.

"The angels which kept not their first estate, but left their own habitation, He hath reserved in everlasting chains under darkness unto the judgment of the great day." (Jude 1:6)

"Are you confident that you yourself are a guide of the blind, a light of them which are in darkness, an instructor of the foolish, a teacher of babes, which have the form of knowledge and of the truth in the law?" (Romans 2: 19- 20)

1. The story of Elisha guiding the blind soldiers to the Light of the world.

2. Kolya Thibault guiding the other eight hikers into darkness. Everybody has a choice to make as to who they're going to follow.

"Now all these things happen unto them for examples: and they are written for our warning, upon whom the ends of the world are come." (1 Corinthians 10:11)

"Touch, not My anointed." (Psalms 105: 15)

DOCUMENTATION / EFFECTS / COMMENTARY

"And the angels which kept not their first estate, but left their own habitation, He has reserved in everlasting chains under darkness unto the judgment of the great day." (Jude 1:6)

> They came from another dimension to earth to corrupt and destroy.

"We wrestle not against flesh and blood, but against principalities, against powers, against the rulers of darkness of this world, against spiritual wickedness in high places." (Ephesians 6:12)

> That evil wickedness in the heavens will come to the earth to destroy.

"Whereas angels, which are greater in power and might, bring not a railing accusation against them before the Lord." (2 Peter 2:11)

> The arguments are over! They are dead! The Creator of all things will destroy them at the great day!

"And there was war in heaven: Michael and his angels fought against the Devil and his angels." (Revelation 12:7)

> That is a supernatural war between angels.

"And prevailed not, neither was their place found any more in heaven." (Revelation 12:8)

> At Christ's return to earth, these angels are destroyed.

"The Devil and his angels are cast out together into this earth before the great day." (Revelation 12:9)

> The devil has a thousand years, called the millennium, locked away in the pit, but the angels are destroyed before the first day of the millennium.]

"And it came to pass when men begin to multiply on the face of the earth, and daughters were born unto them, that the sons of God saw the daughters of men that they were fair; and they took them wives all of which they chose." (Genesis 6: 1-2)

> That was the first intermixing of angels with mankind. It earns them an automatic death sentence from our Creator.

"I beheld Satan as lightning fall from heaven. Behold, I give you power to tread on serpents and scorpions, and over all the power of the enemy:" (Luke 10:18-19)

"Their torment was as the torment of a scorpion, when he strikes a man." (Revelation 9:5)

> The angels know that the Lord gave us power over them, and it would make sense why they would try to mimic a scorpion with Lyuda. A scorpion will pull the victim to its mouth and regurgitate its acids into the victim's mouth. It turns the inside of the victim to mush, and then it sucks it back out again. The nine hikers obviously did not have the power that Christ gave over the Angels.

"Touch not mine anointed." (1 Chronicles 16: 22 + Psalms 105: 15)

"The Lord forbid that I should stretch forth my hand against the Lord's anointed." (1 Samuel 26:11)

> Being a Christian, means you are one of His anointed. Having His knowledge and the Holy Spirit upon you. That is in part what the oil was about in Gideon's lamps. (*See reference:* Isaiah 10: 27 because of the anointing.) Because of the anointing, we have the victory over these fallen angels! Once the Lord's hand comes upon those who touch the Lord's anointed, they learn not to do it again. Or, like the angels, they will go up in smoke.

"O covering cherub - - - I will cast you to the ground, I will lay you before kings, that they may behold you - - - because of the iniquity of your traffic; I will bring forth a fire from the midst of you, it shall devour you, and I will bring you to ashes upon the earth in the sight of all them that behold you. And never shall you be any more." (Ezekiel 28: 16-19). And slaves, and souls of men. (Revelation 18:13)

> Satan is that cherub that will be cast to earth after the war in heaven. The iniquity of his traffic, slaves, and souls of men, is probably much like the human trafficking in this dimension. It's where the theory of his angels competing for lost souls comes from in part. It also shows our Creator as a consuming fire that will devour him, bringing him to ashes so that he goes up in smoke forever, never shall he be anymore.

"For our God is a consuming fire." (Hebrews 12: 29)

> "His children are likened unto stars," Genesis 37: 9-10, which sometimes in heaven a star will go supernova. A comparison to think about.

"Fearful sights and great signs shall there be from heaven, men's hearts failing them for fear, and for looking after those things which are coming on the earth." (Luke 21:11 + 26)

> Alexander Kolevatov's heart seems to have failed him for fear.

"It's a fearful thing to fall into the hands of the living God." (Hebrews 10: 31)

"Submit yourselves therefore to God, resist the devil, and he will flee from you." (James 4:7)

> Satan is the greatest supernatural angel of all angels and is afraid of our Creator.

The Angel of the Lord appeared unto Moses in a flame of fire out of the midst of a bush. And the bush burned with fire, and the bush was not consumed. (Exodus 3:2)

The sons of Aaron offered strange fire before the Lord which he commanded them not to do, and there went out fire from the Lord and devoured them, and they died. (Leviticus 10:1- 2)

I see four men loose, walking in the midst of the fire; and they have no hurt. (Daniel 3: 25)

> This documents that it could be hot as fire inside the tent and yet not consume the tent. This also documents that there's more than one kind of fire.

"After speaking with the Lord, the skin on Moses's face shown, and the people of Israel when they saw that the skin on Moses's face was shining, they were afraid to come near him." (Exodus 34 29-30)

> This shows that there can be skin reactions when coming in contact with the supernatural. It may also be why the pilots wanted those bodies sealed up before they would move the hikers. Again, causing the preservation of the footprints?

"They brought a man with a dumb spirit to Christ, and right away the spirit convulsed him; and he fell on the ground, and rolled about foaming." (Mark 9:18-20)

> They said the foam at the hikers' mouths could've been a result of a seizure or some kind of compression. Evil also can bring this symptom about.

"Christ met a man with an unclean spirit, that no man could put chains or fetters on, because he would break them in pieces." (Mark 5:2-4)

> This documents the superhuman strength of the supernatural.

"As for the likeness of the living creatures, their appearance was like burning coals of fire, and like the appearance of lamps: it went up and down among the living creatures; and the fire was bright, and out of the fire went forth lightning." (Ezekiel 1: 13)

> Appearance of lamps or the lights in the sky, with beams of lightning.

"Suddenly there shined a light around him a light from heaven:" (Acts 9:3)

> A light in the sky.

"Behold the mountain was full horses and chariots of fire round about Elisha." (2 Kings 6:17)

> These chariots of fire are flying vehicles.

"When you hear the sound of My chariots going over the top of the mulberry trees, then you shall know the Lord has gone before you to destroy your enemies." (2 Samuel 5: 24 + 2 King 7:6)

> Both of these events were combined, and paraphrased above to bring forth the knowledge of His chariots destroying our enemies.

"He appeared in another form." (Mark 16:12)

> This documents that the supernatural can take on different forms.

"Then came Jesus, the doors being shut, and stood in the midst." (John 20:26)

> This shows that the spiritual body can walk through things without disturbing the solid objects, which means the angel could walk through snow without leaving footprints.

"But take you heed: behold, I have foretold you all things." Mark 13: 23

> There are no unsolved mysteries with our Heavenly Father! These thousands of years old Manuscripts are where the documentation of this theory to the Dyatlov Pass Incident comes from.

Thanks be, again, to our Heavenly Father who brought it to light.

ABOUT THE AUTHOR

THE RANDLE FAMILY WAS A family of four boys and two girls, in which I was second to the youngest. We were brought up under a strong Christian faith. It meant that if you believe that Christ died for our sins, we would be forgiven and have salvation. But I never understood why this had to be done. When I reached the age of thirty, I was diagnosed as having cancer. It got me listening to a preacher that taught the Bible. Then, it became more clear, as we went through the Bible verse by verse and chapter by chapter, why all this had to be done. It basically gives all His children a way to come back to Him from following a stranger (Satan). Christians also fall to Satan's enticing ways of the world and start following the wrong gods. As a strong Christian family, we are to help them back – Christians as well as non-Christians. So sharing this theory of the sixty-year-old mystery of the nine hikers in Russia, whose government tried to keep His Word from reaching His people in Russia, is what the story is all about: the story of His Passover.

www.ingramcontent.com/pod-product-compliance
Lightning Source LLC
Chambersburg PA
CBHW030156100526
44592CB00009B/301